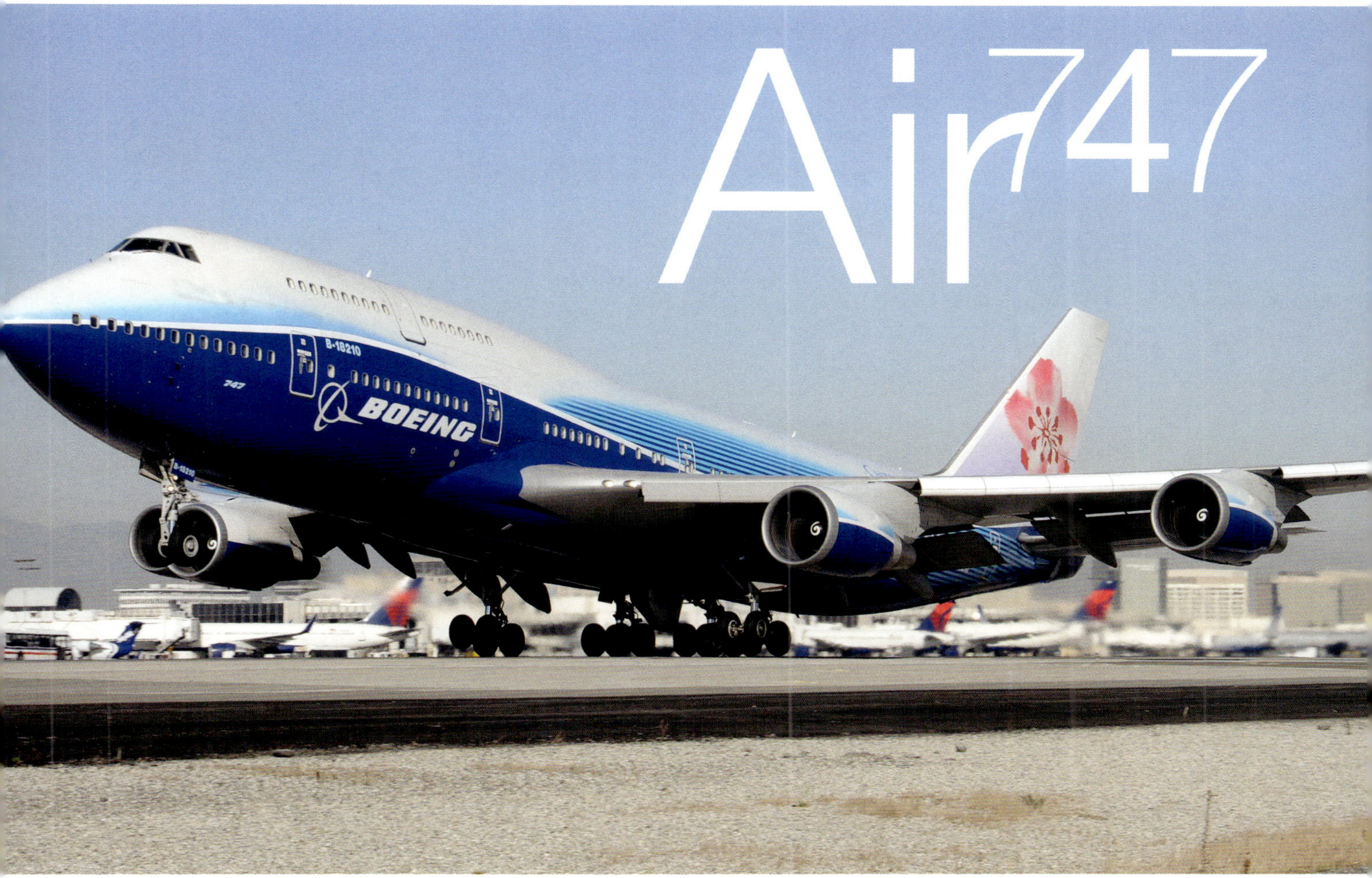

Air 747

Experiencing the Passion: Boeing's Jumbo Jet

Sam Chui and Charles Kennedy

Aviation, to me, has been a lifetime passion. During my journey, I have met many thousands of people who shared the same passion. Many of you have helped me along the way to advance further in aviation. I couldn't possibly achieve all this without your help, support and opportunities given. Aviation connects people of the world and makes the world a better place.

I would like to take this opportunity to say a special thanks to my family, who always has faith in me, in everything I do.

Thanks also to Steve Finnigan, Bhavna Vadher, Sean Maher, Emma Entero and all at Astral Horizon Press and The Airline Boutique for making this project possible.

As always, I am looking forward to your comments and feedback. Thank you so much for your support!

Designed by Simon De Rudder

© 2020 Astral Horizon Press, all rights reserved

www.samchui.com
www.astralhorizon.co.uk
www.theairlineboutique.co.uk

Air747 by Sam Chui and Charles Kennedy
ISBN 978-0-9932604-9-0

Other books by Sam Chui
- Air
- Air 2
- Air 3

Other books by Charles Kennedy
- Air 3
- Haynes Owners Workshop Manual: Boeing 707
- Jetliners Of The Red Star
- DC-8 & The Flying Tiger Line
- Tiger 747
- The Story Of The MD-11

Contents

Experiencing The Passion	5
The Story Of The Boeing 747	7
Korean Air 747-400 And 747-8i	44
Iran Air: Classic 747s Over Persia	50
Mahan Air: Iran's Independent Airline	58
Cathay Pacific: Spirit Of Hong Kong	62
Cathay Pacific: History Special	68
Air-India Maharaja Service	70
Syrian Special Performance	76
My Flight On A Private 747SP	80
Corsair Et Le Jumbo	88
Flying On A KLM 747-400 Combi	94
ANA's Peoplemover: The 747-400D	100
The Emir Of Kuwait's Jumbo	104
Air China Domestic 747-8i	108
Qatar Airways 747-8F Freight Giant	112
Two Flights With Saudia 747-300	118
Lufthansa First Class On Two Jumbos	124
Orient Thai: A Dream Of Siam	134
British Airways: History Special	138
Speedbird 747	142
Qantas And The 747: A Tribute	148
The Last United 747	154
Singapore Girl Says Farewell To The 747	158
Last Flight Of El Al's 747	162
Desert Soliloquy	168
Afterword	174
Experiencing The Passion	175

Experiencing The Passion

What's my favorite aircraft? I get this question a lot. The answer is, of course, the Boeing 747, the Queen of the Skies. It is my first love and it always has my heart. The aircraft is incredibly good looking, elegant, and instantly recognisable around the world. Boeing's Jumbo Jet made the globe smaller and opened up world travel for me.

Growing up in Hong Kong in the pre-digital era, entertainment options were limited. But I did have Kai Tak Airport close by. Every second plane landing or takeoff was a 747. I've spent many hours watching countless 747 making 'the final turn' to land, or speed down the runway on their way to countless exotic locations across the globe.

My first Boeing 747 flight was in 1993, onboard United Airlines Flight 800, a famous flight number inherited from Pan Am, from Hong Kong to Tokyo Narita. It was a brand new 747-400. I was sitting in the rear economy and the plane was huge, like nothing I'd been on before. My love of aviation started with the 747. The excitement walking down the jetbridge to board a 747 was unreal. Watching a 747 taxi so close to the airport fence that I can even wave to passengers inside are some of my favourite past memories. So many unique features of the 747 are found on no other aircraft. Turning left into the nose, the intimate seating on upper deck, and you arrive even before the pilots!

Over the years, I have been fortunate to fly on the 747 nearly 350 times, with every model from the -100, through the rare SP, and up to the latest -8 series even including the -8F freighter. Now, I am proud to share the experience with you. Sit back and relax, and join me on this Air747 journey together.

The Story Of The Boeing 747

Boeing In The Early Years Of Flight

William Edward Boeing, originally Böing, was born in Detroit Michigan on October 1, 1881. His father was a wealthy mining engineer who had immigrated from Hagen-Hohenlimburg, near Dortmund in Germany, and his mother, Marie Ortmann, had immigrated from Vienna. William anglicised his name upon his return to the United States in 1900 to attend Yale after completing his schooling in Vevey, Switzerland. He left without graduating to go into the lumber business, purchasing large amounts of land around Grays Harbour on the Olympic Peninsula near Seattle, in Washington state.

During the Alaska-Yukon-Pacific Exposition of 1909 in Seattle, William Boeing saw an aeroplane flying for the first time; his fascination with boat design quickly changed into a passion that would define his life and ultimately change the world. He went to Los Angeles to learn to fly at the Glenn L. Martin Flying School, and purchased a Martin seaplane known as the Flying Birdcage due to the number of wires holding it together. The seaplane was assembled in Washington state but was soon crashed by one of Boeing's pilots. When it turned out that getting parts up to the Pacific Northwest for the repair would take months, William Boeing opined to his friend George Conrad Westervelt that he could probably build one better himself. ▶

The result of this conversation was the B&W (Boeing & Westervelt) Seaplane, built by their very own fledgling Pacific Aero Products Co, incorporated on July 15, 1916. When the United States entered World War 1 in April 1917, the name of the company was changed to the Boeing Airplane Co., and an order for fifty B&W Seaplanes, also known as the Boeing Model 1, was placed by the US Navy.

After World War 1 was over, a surplus of cheap ex-military aircraft flooded the second-hand market, driving many manufacturers of new aeroplanes out of business. Others got into whatever lines of work could sustain them. In those lean years, serious consideration was given to getting out of the aeroplane business altogether; the Boeing Aircraft Co was put to use making furniture as well as flat-bottomed boats called Sea Sleds.

With the company's main focus remaining with aeroplanes, in the 1920s Boeing built a number of fighters (then known as pursuit, hence the P- prefix) such as the PW-9 and P-12. July 20, 1925 saw the first flight of the Boeing Model 40, a mail plane with seating for four passengers. Boeing Air Transport began running the Model 40 on the mail run from San Francisco to Chicago on July 1, 1927. In a joint venture with Pratt & Whitney, Boeing Air Transport bought Varney Air Lines, National Air Transport, Stout Air Services, and Pacific Air Transport. This merged entity was renamed the United Aircraft And Transport Corporation, or UATC for short, which later became United Airlines. (The lineage of the airlines that were acquired by UATC going back to the early 1920s make it possible for United Airlines to lay claim to being the oldest airline in the United States.)

The dawn of the 1930s saw Boeing make an impressive leap into the future with the B-247, a ten-seat twin-engined all-metal airliner. The first flight took place on February 8, 1933 and entered service on May 22 with United, whose summer 1933 timetable included the fastest method of travelling from coast-to-coast: a daily United B-247 leaving Newark at noon and, after eight en route stops, landing the next morning at San Francisco at 0655 local. The fare was $160 one way ($3,000 in 2020 adjusted for inflation). This was the first time a transcontinental flight was possible without nightstopping at hotels. The B-247 was a pioneer in other ways too, incorporating retractable landing gear, an autopilot, trim tabs, and de-icing boots on the leading edges of the wings and empennage. The fully-cantilevered wing was very ahead of its time, allowing a cruise speed that outpaced the premier US fighter plane of the day (the Boeing P-12), with a landing speed of just 60 knots (100 kilometres per hour). Pilots and mechanics soon discovered that the wing was so effective that the B-247 could be taxied with its tailwheel off the ground at speeds as low as ten miles per hour.

While ownership of United Airlines gave Boeing a captive customer, the temptation to keep rival airlines from buying B-247s was ultimately a handicap. It was Boeing rejecting TWA's order (Transtate and Western Airlines, later Trans World Airlines) for B-247s that drove TWA and others to Douglas, who responded by creating the DC-2 and DC-3, which went on to sell over 16,000 airframes, in contrast to the B-247's 75 (70 of which were for United). In any case, the federal government was looking to stamp out this kind of anti-competitive corporate behaviour, and the passage of the Air Mail Act of 1934 prohibited airlines and manufacturers from being under the same ownership umbrella, so the company was split into three: United Airlines, United Aircraft Technology (the precursor to today's United Technologies), and the Boeing Airplane Company.

In 1933, the Boeing team began work on the huge XB-15 bomber prototype, which, upon its first flight on October 15, 1937, was the biggest aircraft built in the United States. Its intended mission was ultra-long range sorties, covering up to 5,000 miles (8,000 kilometres), which it was able to do, albeit at a crawl – the fastest speed it ever achieved in level flight was 197 miles per hour (317 kilometres per hour). With a 2,000 lb (907 kilogram) payload, an even more laborious 145 miles per hour (233 kilometres per hour) was as good as it got. At those speeds, the 5,000 mile trip lasted a stultifying 33 hours of flight. Thus the XB-15 project was abandoned as being not fit for combat operation, but led to the B-314 Clipper flying boat, which first flew on June 7, 1938, with an order for six aircraft from

Pan American World Airways, the "chosen instrument" of United States aviation overseas and a by-word for innovation, quality and style.

Route-proving began on February 23, 1939. Pan Am put the huge flying boat formally into service on March 29 on Foreign Air Mail Route #14, San Francisco to Hong Kong via Honolulu, Guam, and Manila. The entire trip from end to end took six days. Atlantic crossings by Clipper began on June 24, from New York to Southampton via Shediac (New Brunswick), Botwood (Newfoundland) and Foynes (Ireland). The standard of luxury on Pan American's Boeing 314s has rarely been matched on heavier-than-air transport since: the aircraft incorporated a lounge and dining area, and the galleys were crewed by chefs from four-star hotels. Men and women were provided with separate dressing rooms, and white-coated stewards served five- and six-course meals with silver service. The product was matched by the price: New York to Southampton round-trip was $675, equivalent to $12,550 in 2020, and San Francisco to Hong Kong round-trip was $1,368, a whopping $25,400 in 2020.

Flying was reduced due to the outbreak of World War 2 just months later, but the Atlantic services continued to neutral Lisbon and Foynes in Ireland for the duration of the war, as well as missions for the War and Navy Departments including supply flights to West Africa and even as far as Russia. Franklin D. Roosevelt flew to the Casablanca Conference aboard the Pan Am-crewed Dixie Clipper.

(At the outbreak of the war in the Pacific, one of Pan Am's B-314s, the Pacific Clipper, was en route to New Zealand. Rather than risk flying back to Honolulu and being shot down by Japanese fighters, it was decided to fly west to New York. In one of the great aviation adventures of all time, the Pacific Clipper set out from Auckland on December 8, 1941 and flew over 31,500 miles (50,694 km) via Surabaya, Karachi, Bahrain, Khartoum and Leopoldville, landing at the LaGuardia Field seaplane base in New York harbour on the morning of January 6, 1942.)

After the war, the Clippers were obsolete – their advantage was that they did not require runways (or even good visibility – in foggy conditions they could land out at sea and taxi into harbour), but in the course of the war, long runways were built around the world to accommodate heavy bombers. The fleet was removed from service by Pan Am in 1946 and the seven surviving machines were purchased by New World Airways and moored for the next four years in San Diego awaiting a new mission that never materialised, and were scrapped in 1950.

In a similar timeframe, Boeing created the four-engined B-307 Stratoliner, also for Pan Am but for operations on land, seating 38 passengers (or 25 in beds). The first flight of the Stratoliner took place on December 31, 1938, although the aircraft crashed during a demonstration of asymmetrical power, killing all ten aboard, including Boeing's chief engineer, chief aerodynamicist, and test pilots from TWA, Dutch airline KLM, and Boeing. Despite this tragic loss, the programme continued with an initial delivery to TWA founder Howard Hughes who intended to beat his own round-the-world record, an attempt that was abandoned due to the Nazi Germany invasion of Poland. The first airline deliveries of B-307s were in early 1940, to TWA for nonstop flights between New York and Los Angeles, and to Pan Am for flights from Miami down to Latin and South America. In the late 1940s the surviving Stratoliners were sold to small operators such as French carrier Aigle Azur, who used them on routes to Vietnam, then a French colonial possession, where they remained in service with different local operators until 1974, and the Haitian Air Force.

During the war, Boeing's main output was heavy bombers such as the B-17 Flying Fortress (12,731 produced) and the B-29 Superfortress (3,970 produced + 847 reverse-engineered Tupolev Tu-4s). The B-29 was commercially more significant because, as the most expensive weapons system developed by the United States in the war, exceeding the cost of the Manhattan Project by nearly two billion dollars, it was the beneficiary of the latest state-of-the-art technology, including a fully pressurised cabin and dual-wheel tricycle undercarriage.

▲ A majestic Pan Am Stratocruiser in the golden age of the propliner (Pan Am Flight Academy)

The Boeing C-97 tanker transport added an upper deck running the length of the aircraft to the B-29 platform. The first flight was on November 9, 1944, and the machine went on to sell 811 KC-97 tankers and 77 C-97 transports, remaining in service with the USAF Strategic Air Command until 1978, with two still flying today – one as a waterbomber and one as a privately-owned warbird.

The civilian version of the C-97 was dubbed the B-377 Stratocruiser, a luxurious 84 seat landplane successor to the B-314 Clipper, complete with a downstairs lounge reached by a spiral staircase, a Boeing design flourish that would become much more famous in another airliner a couple of decades hence. Juan T. Trippe, founder and president of Pan Am, had a very high regard for Boeing products because of the Clipper flying boats, and ordered 20 Stratocruisers on November 29, 1945. The first machine took to the air on July 8, 1947, and after a test programme using three aircraft covering a quarter of a million miles (402,000 kilometres), Pan Am began airline service on April 5, 1949, from San Francisco to Honolulu. By the end of the year, Pan Am, British Overseas Airways Corporation (BOAC) and American Airlines (as AOA, American Overseas Airlines) were all flying their B-377s transatlantic, and Northwest Orient within the United States. By the early fifties Pan Am were flying as far east as Beirut and as far west as Hong Kong, Singapore and Sydney. The Stratocruiser represented the last word in propliner luxury, and operated at speeds that were a significant improvement on its predecessors, covering San Francisco to Honolulu in nine hours and 45 minutes, and Tokyo to Honolulu in 11 hours.

The world was about to change. The peace dividend that followed the end of the war paid out in countless ways, as the young engineers and research laboratories were freed from their wartime roles and set about inventing the future, in the form of domestic automation, big cars with fins, colour movies, and LP records. The fifty-sixth and final Stratocruiser rolled off the production line in Seattle and was handed over to BOAC in May 1950. Boeing engineer Wellwood Beall flew to England on the delivery flight, and returned with news and first-hand experience of perhaps the greatest element of the peace dividend of them all – the world's first civilian jetliner, the de Havilland Comet.

▲ The de Havilland Comet was the world's first jetliner to enter service. This is the prototype Comet 2

The Jet Age

The whine of the jet engine was not a novelty in the 1950s, as Maxime Guilliame had patented the idea of using a turbine to power an aircraft as early as 1921, and Alan Arnold Griffith published the ground-breaking An Aerodynamic Theory Of Turbine Design in 1926 for the Royal Aircraft Establishment. Fellow Brit Frank Whittle worked through the thirties developing axial compressor designs, but the simultaneous efforts of Hans von Ohain in Germany meant the first jet aircraft to fly was the Heinkel He-178 on August 27, 1939. The Messerschmitt Me-262 followed it into the air on July 18, 1942 and entered service as the world's first operational jet-powered fighter in April 1944. The Brits were right behind, with the Gloster Meteor entering service with the Royal Air Force (RAF) in July of the same year.

With World War 2 still raging, the government of the United Kingdom formed the Brabazon Committee to determine the UK's civil airliner requirements in the post-war phase. Various jet-powered configurations were considered, from small airmail carriers to passenger jetliners, and in December 1945 BOAC ordered ten De Havilland DH 106 omets. The world's first jet airliner flight was a 31 minute sortie in the evening summer sunshine of July 27, 1949 out of Hatfield in the northern suburbs of London, under the command of John 'Cat's Eyes' Cunningham (a famous World War 2 ace), along with co-pilot Harold 'Tubby' Waters, engineers John Wilson (electrics), Frank Reynolds (hydraulics), and Tony Fairbrother (test observer). After two years of intense test flying, the first production aircraft, G-ALYP (known as 'Yoke Peter' in the phonetic alphabet of the era) first flew on January 9, 1951 and was handed over to BOAC's Comet Unit for test flying, training, and route trials.

The world's first jet-powered revenue flight took place on May 2, 1952 from London to Johannesburg, with five stops en route. By the summer of 1953 BOAC was operating eight jet departures a week out of London — three to Johannesburg, two to Tokyo, two to Singapore, and one to Colombo, with many stops en route. Rome, Beirut, Basra, Karachi, Rangoon, Cairo, Hong Kong, Nairobi, Blantyre... Global mass transit was on its way.

Alas, being a pioneer often exacts a punishing price. After three mid-air break-ups, the Comet 1 was permanently grounded in April 1954. A massive investigation that pushed the barriers of science, especially in the field of metallurgy, revealed the aircraft skin and structure were under-engineered to handle the demands of pressurisation in high altitude flight.

Meanwhile, the USA was about to make its own great leap into the jet age. The undisputed leader in civil airline transports was the Douglas Aircraft Corporation, thanks to the DC-3 (16,079 produced) and their post-war DC-4, DC-6 and DC-7 four-engined propliners (a total of 2,290 produced including military variants). Boeing had extensive jet experience with their B-47 Stratojet bomber; their custom-built proof-of-concept jet transport prototype, the Boeing 367-80 (known informally as the Dash Eighty) took to the air on July 15, 1954.

Although the Dash Eighty most closely resembled the requirements of the US Air Force, who went on to order 803 KC-135/C-135 tanker/transports, the airlines took notice, and by widening and stretching the fuselage, the Boeing 707 was born, first flying on December 20, 1957. Pan Am ordered 20, followed by other US majors such as American Airlines, Continental Airlines, and TWA, plus Australia's Qantas. Following this lead, the major airlines of the world queued up to buy 707s – or the Douglas entry in the jet race, the similarly-configured DC-8.

Seven Oh Heaven

The first revenue Boeing 707 flight was operated by Pan Am on October 26, 1958, from New York's Idlewild airport (later JFK) to Paris Le Bourget, with a fuel stop in Gander, Newfoundland (westbound flights bound for the United States techstopped in Keyflavik, Iceland). As deliveries from Boeing continued, the 707 spread to more and more Pan Am Atlantic routes, such as London Heathrow, Rome, and further afield – Beirut, Tehran, Karachi, and Bombay to the east, and Honolulu, Anchorage, Tokyo, and Hong Kong to the west.

▲ Boeing's proof-of-concept jet transport testbed was designated the 367-80, known as the Dash Eighty, and led to the 707 (Boeing)

Early adopters included American Airlines, who introduced their 707s on the Los Angeles to New York route on January 25, 1959, Qantas (the first export customer), Sabena (the first carrier in Europe), Lufthansa, Air France, Air-India, South African Airways, Varig, and many others. The power of the jet turbine slashed travel times on the world's major air routes in half.

De Havilland worked to fix the problems of the Comet 1, and while doing so, stretched the original design to add capacity, swapped the in-house de Havilland Ghost engines for Rolls-Royce Avons to add performance, and fitted extra fuel tanks to add range. The updated Comet 4 won the battle of the Atlantic on

▲ Biman Bangaldesh operated a fleet of ex-Northwest Orient 707-351Cs on long haul flights to Europe in the 1970s and 1980s (Guy Van Herbruggen collection)

▲ Ecuatoriana's 720s were among the most colourful jets ever seen (Guy Van Herbruggen collection)

October 4, 1958, by beating the 707 into service by 22 days on the London to New York route.

But ultimately the Comet 4 lost the war. Despite being a safe and reliable craft, the Comet 4 could not compete with the 707. Even in its early -100 incarnation, the 707 was able to seat 110 in a typical two-class configuration with a maximum takeoff weight of 247,000 pounds (112,037 kg), whereas the Comet 4 could seat only 56 in a two-class cabin with a maximum takeoff weight of 156,000 pounds (70,760 kilograms).

Jets Go Short Haul

With the market for jet transports linking major cities of the world sewn up, Boeing shifted its attention to the next market segment, short and medium haul flights between smaller cities. By shrinking the 707, they added a new type to their product line – the 720. It was the first jet to serve many of the ports it served, and for seven of the 16 delivery customers that bought 720s, it was their first turbine-powered aircraft.

United operated the world's first revenue service by a 720 on July 5, 1960, when N7201U, configured with 44 first class and 53 economy (or 'coach') seats, flew from Los Angeles to Chicago via Denver; American Airlines followed on July 31 with their trademark 'Jet Gateway' service out of Cleveland to Los Angeles via St Louis.

Engine technology was advancing at a fast rate, and Pratt & Whitney evolved their already successful JT3C turbojet into the JT3D turbofan, which was quieter, more efficient and more powerful, especially at low speeds. Boeing offered the new engine option for aircraft on order, as well as conversions for existing JT3C powered machines. Turbofan equipped 707s and 720s were suffixed with a "B", creating the 707-120B, 707-320B, and 720B. Even the Dash 80 prototype was reengined, and thus became a 367-80B. Pilot feedback said the new powerplants were like adding a fifth engine.

A jetliner dedicated to the short- and medium-haul market temporarily covered by the 720 was needed to serve the hundreds, indeed thousands of secondary towns and cities with jet speed. If building the hardware to link the world's top 50 cities was profitable, imagine building the hardware to link the next couple of thousand. In early discussions with the US majors, United, Eastern and American all wanted different things – four engines for United because of its high-elevation hub at Denver, three engines at Eastern to cover its overwater legs in the Caribbean and Gulf of Mexico, and just two engines for American for efficiency.

De Havilland in Britain were working on the three-engined Trident, and collaborated with Boeing to the extent that the paper 727 was to be powered by Rolls-Royce Spey engines built in the United States under licence by Allison as the AR963, although Boeing soon decided to go their own way. De Havilland bowed so readily to the demands of Britain's state-owned carrier, British European Airways, that the Trident was incompatible with the needs of virtually all other markets and was an export dodo, with a total of only 117 built, the vast majority for BEA (who became British Airways in 1974).

Unopposed, the 727 began test flying on February 9, 1963, receiving a telegram of congratulations from the Kennedy White House, and went into service on February 9, 1964 with Eastern Airlines, and was an immediate sales smash hit. The 727 was a big step up in terms of its performance, demonstrated by incredible short field capability. This was the first jetliner in the world to be built with the expectation of routinely operating off 5,000 foot (1,500 metre) runways.

To do so, the 727 relied on sophisticated high-lift wing flaps which also generated large amounts of drag. This overtaxed some pilots coming onto jets from more sedate prop-driven craft, who underestimated how easy it was to get the 727 to start sinking fast on approach. Four 727s suffered identical crashes on landing – United 389, American 383, United 227, and All Nippon 060 – which killed 264 people between September 1965 and the start of 1966. The Comet wasn't the only pioneer to have a troubled introduction to service, albeit there was nothing wrong with the 727 except that it had to be flown according to the manual. (Air travel in the 1960s in general was a far more dangerous pursuit than it is today, with the Nippon crash on February 4 being the

▲ This ex-Northwest Orient Airlines 727 had a second life in Peru with AeroContinente

first of five air disasters in Japan in 1966, two of which happened on the same day – CPAir crashing on landing at Haneda and hours later a BOAC 707 breaking up in severe clear air turbulence having just taxied past the still-smouldering DC-8, bringing the one-day death toll for the Tokyo area to 188, and 376 in Japan for the year. And that was just Japan.)

The run of accidents was a wake-up call to standardise pilot training and aircraft operations – bearing in mind senior airline pilots flying jets in the 1960s were only a few years younger than the Wright Brothers themselves. It was incredible to think how far heavier-than-air flight had come in such a short time.

Boeing decided to double-down on 'small is beautiful' and created the twin-engined baby of the line, the 737, which still managed to retain eighty percent commonality with the 707 but with a seating capacity of less than 100. The first flight of a 737-100 took place on April 9, 1967 and entered service with Lufthansa on February 10, 1968. Some updates and a slight stretch created the second chapter of what is known as the "737 Original", the 737-200, although sales dynamite for the 737 was still a few decades in the future, selling only a few dozen per year in the late 1960s and 1970s.

While the 737 was a bit of a problem child for the Boeing sales team, the 7C7 was being produced in record numbers: 77 in 1966, 112 in 1967, and another 111 in 1968. Boeing couldn't build 727s fast enough: 134 in 1966, 154 in 1967 and 161 in 1968.

The 1960s was the first full decade of the jet age, and the future path of hardware evolution was unwritten. The British and French were committing the vast majority of their national aviation industries to the joint development of the supersonic Concorde, capable of crossing the Atlantic in just three hours, and the Americans were doing much the same with supersonic paper aeroplanes such as the swing-wing Boeing B-733, B-2707 and Lockheed L-500.

That said, American airframers also had an eye for economies of scale and efficiency, with two widebody jumbos under development: McDonnell Douglas with the DC-10 and Lockheed with the L-1011 both in California, and up the West Coast in Seattle.

▲ The 747 was two-and-a-half times bigger than the 707 it replaced (Boeing)

The Genesis Of The 747

With a fleet of over 100 Boeing 707s, Pan Am flew out of US coastal cities – New York, San Francisco, Miami, Los Angeles, Boston – to five other continents excluding only Antarctica, and defined the jet age more than any other carrier. With traffic rising ten percent every year, the need for a bigger plane was obvious.

The US Department of Defense issued a request designated CX-HLS (Heavy Logistics System) for proposals to fulfil its need for a heavy lifter. The fuselage width was determined by the need to carry military vehicles in pairs, side-by-side. Douglas, Lockheed and Boeing were all asked to submit proposals, and after considerable scrutiny, the Lockheed bid was selected, which became the C-5A Galaxy.

Boeing's efforts were not in vain. Pan Am's president, Juan T. Trippe, went on a now-legendary fishing trip with Boeing's president, William M. Allen. Each threw down the gauntlet to the other. Of a new supersized peoplemover, "If you build it, we'll buy it," promised Trippe; "If you buy it, we'll build it," promised Allen.

Malcom T. Stamper, who joined Boeing in 1962, was tapped by Allen to spearhead the 747 programme. (Stamper would go on to be Boeing's longest-serving president, and in 1978 become one of the first executives in the United States to be paid more than one million dollars a year.) Stamper appointed Joseph 'Joe' Sutter to be the project manager of the design team.

Various configurations were considered, such as a double-decker 707, and a side-by-side double-bubble fuselage. Airlines were generally negative about these improvised solutions, and Boeing also had to consider compatibility with the airfreight industry. At that time, in the mid-1960s, it was assumed that the future of passenger air travel would be supersonic, and Boeing were still pouring a fantastic amount of resources into the Mach 3 swing-wing B-2707; the 747's future was expected to be mostly as a freighter, and that even early passenger models would be converted to haul freight.

To establish the width of the 747 fuselage, the dimensions of two standard main deck containers were placed side-by-side and a circle was drawn around them. The cockpit was moved up to a bubble above the main deck to make more room for cargo, with space abaft for avionics and crew rest. That is, until Juan

▲ Roll out for the 747 prototype, September 30, 1968 (Boeing)

Trippe paid Boeing's plywood mock-up a visit in March 1966 and marked out the space upstairs for a cocktail lounge. Boeing repurposed the spiral staircase that had led down to the bar on the B-377 Stratocruiser and an icon of air travel was born.

Boeing needed a plant in which to build the 747. After surveying 50 sites around the country, in June 1966 they took out an option to buy a 780-acre site next to a military base at Paine Field, near Everett in Washington State. Malcolm Stamper oversaw the construction of the new facility, which turned out to be an enormous undertaking – more than 30.5 million cubic metres of earth had to be moved, and to get the 34,000 tons of structural steel to the site, a railway spur was built which included the second-steepest gradient in the United States. Construction was hampered by a record-breaking 67 consecutive days of rain, which brought flooding and mudslides and added an unanticipated additional cost of $5 million.

The full-size 747 mock-up was built before the factory roof above it was completed. The first production employees were in the factory at the start of 1967, which had an internal capacity of 5.8 million cubic metres, the biggest building in the world, taking the crown by two million cubic metres from the cathedral-like Vertical Assembly Building at the Kennedy Space Center on the tropical Atlantic coast of Florida, used to stack the Saturn V rockets for trips to the Moon.

By May 1967, most of the major tooling was installed and the prototype was under construction. Parts and assemblies began arriving in August from subcontractors such as Northrop (40 sub-assembly panels for the rear fuselage), North American (fibreglass/alloy wing leading edges), Fairchild-Hiller (leading and trailing edge flaps, control surfaces), and other Boeing facilities (such as wing spars and skin panels from the factory in Auburn, 20 miles south of Everett). The young plane builders who were bringing the 747 dream into reality were contemporaries of the Apollo space workers and in the same league of engineering prowess and high energy levels, and worked at such a pace and in such punishing conditions that they became known as The Incredibles, working all hours in a plant that was initially without even a roof or heat.

As the first aircraft, registered N7470, neared completion, its weight crept upwards, threatening to exceed the two percent margin allowed under the contract with Pan Am; the maximum takeoff weight rose from 680,000 pounds (308,442 kilograms) to 710,000 pounds (322,050 kilograms). It was calculated that every 1,000 pounds (454 kilograms) of extra structural weight would cost Pan Am $5,000 per aircraft per year in lost payload. The early Pratt & Whitney JT9D jet engine, already at or beyond the state of the art for powerplants of the time, was spec'd to produce 41,000 pounds (182kN) of thrust; with the increased weight of the plane, it would somehow need to generate an extra 1,000 pounds (4.45 kN) of thrust.

The engine in particular was proving to be a problem. The first JT9D was test-run in early December 1966 at the Pratt & Whitney facility in East Hartford Connecticut, and a Boeing B-52 was appropriated as a flying test bed with a single JT9D installed in place of a pair of J-57s. The most serious shortcoming was that the 46 blades of the first-stage fan were rubbing against the bottom of the engine casing, and the casing itself was being bent out of shape from a perfect circle into a slight oval at high power settings in flight. The friction with the whirling fans resulted in power surges and explosive compressor stalls.

Efforts to lose weight with broad strokes didn't get far. Reducing the triple-slotted trailing edge flaps to double-slotted meant an unacceptably high approach speed; making the two main body gears non-steerable required the use of asymmetric power during taxiing, which resulted in a stationwagon full of observers being blown over by the jet efflux off the runway (the body gear steering was put back on). Some smaller savings were found here and there, but the weight issue and

▲ First flight of the 747, with the Boeing company F-86 chase plane alongside, February 9, 1969   (Boeing)

the lack of thrust available from early engines was never really solved; the early 747-100s were heavy and underpowered.

The financial cost of the 747 became so punishing that new Boeing president Thorton 'T' Wilson, who took over from Bill Allen on April 28, 1968, had to make 60,000 employees redundant, half of them production workers, despite orders for nearly 200 747s from 26 airlines. Pan Am president Juan Trippe too was entering his sunset years, and handed control of Pan Am to a new chairman, Harold Gray, who in the summer of 1968 gave the programme a boost by converting eight more options for 747s into firm sales, bringing Pan Am's order up to 33 aircraft. The scale of Pan Am's commitment was demonstrated by a gigantic investment at New York's JFK airport including upgrading the Worldport terminal and the construction of a huge 747 maintenance facility.

Into The Air

The 747 prototype was rolled out under soggy grey skies on September 30, 1968, with a performance of Elgar's Pomp And Circumstance march by the Everett High School band, half an hour of speeches, followed by the hangar doors opening to reveal the gigantic white jumbo adorned with a red cheatline and the logos of its first 26 airline customers. Once N7470 had been tugged clear of the hangar, flight attendants from the customer airlines were given rather vague instructions about exactly when they should crack their bottles of champagne against the side of the aeroplane, resulting in a chaotic christening that was nonetheless good-spirited, while a 707, a 727 and a 737 passed low overhead, skirting just under the cloud base.

Test pilot Jack Waddell, who flew for North American Aviation before joining Boeing in 1957, was selected to lead the test flying programme. He chose Brien Wygle to be his co-pilot, who had just finished up as chief test pilot on the 737. Riding sideways on the flight engineer's panel would be ace flight test engineer Jesse Wallick (and from an impressive family – Jesse's brother Lew Wallick was a Boeing test pilot on the first flights of the XB-47D, 720, 727, 737, 747SP, 757 and 767.)

At the end of January 1968, the 747 was released to Flight Ops and N7470 began taxi and high speed runs. Heavy test equipment and water ballast in beer kegs was installed, and mailbags in the rear of the main deck brought the first flight weight up to 476,000 pounds (215,909 kilograms).

Jack Waddell had two concerns – firstly that the engines, still an unknown quantity, would suffer serious compressor stalls and lose power as the aircraft pitched skyward, and worse, that all four would do so simultaneously, not only robbing the aircraft of thrust but also of hydraulic power to drive the flight controls. Therefore the prototype was fitted with electrical back-up power driven by a large bank of batteries to ensure the hydraulic systems remained pressurised and usable even in the event of the failure of all four engines. The other concern was landing the plane with the cockpit so high above the ground, and so Boeing engineers constructed a mock-up of the flight deck and mounted it 29 feet (8.84 metres) up on a rig that was towed around the airfield by a truck to familiarise Waddell with the grandstand view.

February 9, 1969 was chosen for the 747's debut flight. The big day dawned grey and cloudy, but Waddell spoke by radio to the crew of a 707 airborne on a pre-delivery test flight in the local area and ascertained the weather was flyable. Bill Allen walked out with the crew to N7470 and told Waddell, "Jack, I hope you understand that the future of the company rides with you guys this morning." No pressure!

The first engine was started at 11:09am and a few minutes later first officer Wygle called up for taxi clearance. Waddell ordered the F-86 Sabre chaseplane into the air. At 11:35am N7470 was at the runway threshold. "Four stable engines!" announced flight engineer Wallick and the brakes were released. After rolling just 4,500 feet (1,371 metres), the nose was off the ground, and a second later, the jumbo jet was climbing away. Waddell rolled the machine into a 270 degree left turn to pass overhead the field for the benefit of the assembled photographers, then climbed away to get to know Boeing's new flagship.

The crew tried flying with different hydraulic systems shut down and encountered no difficulty. Asymmetric thrust settings were easily tuned out using the flight controls, and kicking a rudder pedal to induce a Dutch Roll (divergent side-to-side roll) had no negative effect. However, when the flaps were extended from 25 to 35 degrees, there was a thump and some vibration. The flaps were raised back up to 25 degrees and Wallick went back to take a look, returning to announce that a section of the flaps on the right wing had come loose. It was time to head back to Everett, although not before a company 727 with Bill Allen and members of the press aboard caught up with N7470 for some air-to-air photos. After one hour and 16 minutes, the first flight of the 747 ended with a safe landing back at base.

Minor repairs to the flaps were made and N7470's second flight took place six days later, lasting two hours and 18 minutes. The third flight was a quick 23 minute sortie to check flap handling and an item on the main landing gear. Bill Allen went for a ride on February 24 for the quick transit across the Seattle area from Everett to Boeing Field where the test programme continued.

The second 747 to fly, and first production 747-121, was N747PA, destined for Pan Am. Clipper Young America rolled out on February 28 and flew for the first time on April 11, to be used in the test programme to evaluate propulsion, fuel, electro-mechanical and avionics systems. N731PA Clipper Bostonian first flew on May 10 to test function and reliability; TWA's first 747-131, N93101, first flew on May 22 to test aerodynamics, stability and control, and N732PA Clipper Storm King joined the test programme starting on July 10, to check flight loads on the structure and surfaces.

N731PA had proved itself to be the most reliable airframe/powerplant combination, and was thus chosen for the 747's international debut at the Paris 1969 Air Salon. The flight hopped over to Seattle's Sea-Tac international airport to pick up fuel and make use of the 12,000 foot (3,657 metre) runway for the nine-hour, 18-minute overnight Atlantic crossing which arrived at Le Bourget on the morning of June 3 to a heroes' welcome. An overheating engine had to be shut down 140 miles (225 kilometres) from Seattle on the return leg but the aircraft had proved itself to be able to take long haul operations in its stride.

The only serious incident to befall a 747 during the test programme took place on December 13, 1969, when N732PA was landing at Boeing's Renton facility to have its test equipment removed and replaced with an airline interior. The short (5,280 foot/1,609 metre) runway and gusting crosswind intimidated the pilot into coming in too low, and the main landing gear clipped an earth bank on the shore of Lake Washington 20 feet (six metres) short of the runway threshold, buckling parts of the landing gear on one side and dragging engines three and four along the tarmac in a shower of sparks and smoke. Repairs took six months and the pilot was fired.

Overall the test programme was incredibly successful, completed in a year and without any major surprises. The enormous 747 was an incredibly stable and flyable aircraft, and dependable in all flight regimes. The Incredibles had done an incredible job.

On the same day as the Renton smash-up, on December 13, 1969 N733PA Clipper Young America was flown from Everett to the Bahamas then up to New York on its delivery flight from Boeing to Pan Am. First Lady Pat Nixon christened the plane in a ceremony on the tarmac at Washington Dulles airport on January 15, 1970, and the stage was set for introduction to service.

Into Service

The 747's inaugural scheduled passenger flight set sail from the Worldport at New York JFK to London Heathrow on the evening of January 21, 1970; in command of N733PA was Captain Bob Weeks, Pan Am's New York base chief pilot. After problems with doors and cargo loading, the engines refused to co-operate, overheating and backfiring due to the gusty wind conditions on the icy tarmac. N733PA finally had four stable engines at 7:29pm and taxied out. Before reaching the runway, however, engine number four overheated and the aircraft returned to the gate, unloading 336 passengers back into the Worldport.

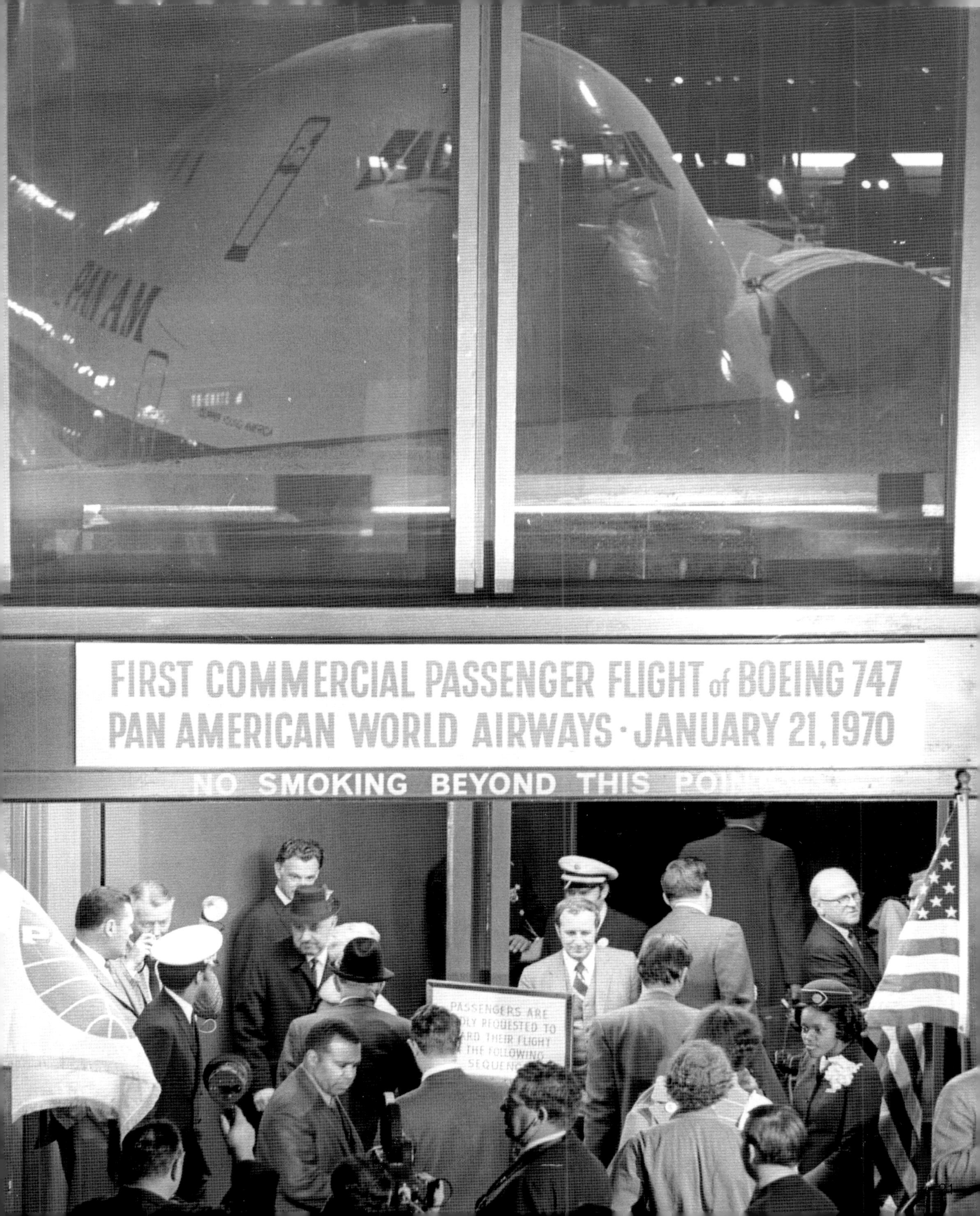
PAN AM
FIRST COMMERCIAL PASSENGER FLIGHT of BOEING 747
PAN AMERICAN WORLD AIRWAYS · JANUARY 21, 1970
NO SMOKING BEYOND THIS POI
PASSENGERS ARE
REQUESTED TO
THEIR FLIGHT
THE FOLLOWING
SEQUEN

Luckily Pan Am had N736PA Clipper Victor on the premises, having been delivered the day before. With the catering and baggage transferred to the new aircraft, the flight finally taxied out at 1:30am in the early hours of the next morning and got airborne at 1:50am. Six hours and 16 minutes later, the flight made an early-afternoon arrival at Heathrow. Not the dawn arrival scheduled perhaps, but without further incident. The age of the jumbo jet had arrived and the world would never be the same.

In March 1970 TWA and American Airlines both began 747 service on the New York to Los Angeles run. Lufthansa put their first 747 on the route from Frankfurt to New York, the 747's first foreign operator. Continental Airlines began flying from Los Angeles to Honolulu in June and a second non-US carrier, Japan Airlines, started Tokyo to Hong Kong and then across the Pacific to Los Angeles. July belonged to Northwest Orient who debuted their 747s on a combination of domestic and transpacific flying: New York to Chicago, Chicago to Seattle and Seattle to Tokyo. Sabena, Air France and Aer Lingus were other early jumbo operations.

As the first 747 deliveries to UK longhaul flag carrier BOAC loomed, labour problems meant that pilots refused to start training until the dispute was settled. The first jumbo for BOAC and the twenty-third built was G-AWNA, flown into London Heathrow on April 22, 1970, followed by G-AWNB on May 6 and G-AWNC on May 28. However the machines were parked and stored while the dispute rumbled on.

Teething Troubles

This saved BOAC a considerable headache, as the early Pratt & Whitney JT9D engines on the 747-100 remained extremely unreliable in service. Just as on Pan Am's inaugural flight, the engines would routinely overheat during start up and taxi, and at high power settings the entire engine cowling would slightly deform, causing rough running and, to the horror of passengers, explosive compressor stalls which, while not particularly dangerous, manifested themselves in the form of bowel-loosening bangs and shooting flames, and countless cancelled flights.

BOAC was able to bypass these teething problems because of its labour problems, and even leasing some of their own stock of this troubled engine to other operators who desperately needed them as their own spares were rapidly exhausted. It wasn't until early 1971 when contracts with pilots and cabin crew were settled and all nominated staff reported for training on March 1, with BOAC 747s getting airborne on passenger services out of the UK on Sunday April 25, with the inaugural flight heading to New York JFK, followed by other early destinations such as Montreal and Bermuda.

Pan Am was more than the launch customer, it was the catalyst for the 747, but like many pioneers, did not flourish the way its successors did. 33 747s was a lot to swallow even for The World's Most Experienced Airline, especially with the price of fuel leaping in 1973, which didn't just make the cost of a flying operation much more expensive, but also suppressed passenger demand, as high gasoline and heating prices soaked up discretionary income across the whole population.

Pan Am couldn't fail on the big routes such as New York to London or San Francisco to Tokyo, and most notably, put the jumbo on their prestigious round-the-world flight, PA001 (San Francisco to New York via Tokyo, Hong Kong, Bangkok, Delhi, Tehran, Beirut, Istanbul, Frankfurt and London) and PA002 (New York to San Francisco with the same stopping points in reverse order), with full traffic rights between all ports.

This is probably the apex of the Jet Age – imagine perhaps a young-ish and successful academic, fighting through lunchtime traffic in Delhi (rickshaws, millions of bicycles, hand-drawn carts and sacred cows) after delivering a scientific lecture, to jump on a Pan Am 747 up to Beirut (then known as the Paris Of The Middle East) to catch up with an old girlfriend. Strong cocktail in the upper deck lounge over the Persian Gulf, chatting with the Iranian ambassador recalled from the royal court of Thailand on his way home to Tehran, and the manager of a very famous rock band flying all the way through to London, but who is already badly drunk. The flimsy flight

Step into The Spacious Age.

When the Boeing 747 superjet enters regular service this winter, you will be able to step into the largest, most luxurious, most spacious jetliner ever built.

You will enter through one of ten wide doors. You will move down broad aisles in a cabin 20 feet wide and 8 feet high.

In economy as well as first class sections, your seat will be extra large, extra comfortable, with plenty of room around and above you.

In first class, you may ascend a spiral staircase to a luxurious lounge where you can relax, walk around and pass the time in the sky.

When your 747 flight takes off, four of the world's most powerful but quiet commercial jet engines will lift you gracefully into the air. Then you can settle back and enjoy the comfort of your living room in a trip across continents or oceans.

The Boeing 747 and The Spacious Age are here.

BOEING 747

These airlines have already ordered Boeing 747s:
Air Canada, Air France, Air India, Alitalia, American, BOAC, Braniff, Continental, Delta, Eastern, El Al, Iberia, Irish, JAL, KLM, Lufthansa, National, Northwest, Pan Am, Qantas, SAS, Sabena, South African, Swissair, TWA, United, World.

▲ The oldest 747 flying, this -131F was delivered to TWA in September 1971 and sold to the Iranian Air Force in November 1975, who still fly it today

deck door is open and the flight crew regularly step out to chat with the cabin crew. Downstairs, the economy class cabin, spaciously configured with just nine-abreast seating, is half empty, and many passengers have a row of seats to themselves. Other than the blue fug of cigarette smoke, it's a very nice way to fly.

Alas, it was not very profitable. Pan Am's vast route network, taking in not only the aforementioned ports of the PA1/2 round-the-world service, also visited the likes of Monrovia, Kinshasa, Saigon, Bali, and Damascus, was better suited to the much smaller 707. Additionally, Pan Am's 747s, having been the first into service, were now the oldest. Every other 747 customer got better aeroplanes, as the design got lighter, stronger, incorporated aerodynamic hacks, and the engines got more efficient.

In addition, the shard-eyed reader will have spotted the continental gap that precluded PA1/2 from being a true round-the-world flight – Pan Am still didn't have domestic traffic rights within the United States, and the lack of domestic feed at its international gateways was another element that made its jumbos hard to fill.

In Service In The USA

Among the most enthusiastic early customers for the 747 were the US domestic-only trunk lines. To start with the least committed effort; Eastern Airlines, in the 1970s the world's biggest airline outside of the USSR's monolithic Aeroflot, didn't go all-in for the jumbo, cancelling their own order in favour of short leases from Pan Am's fleet. Later they tried leasing a pair of 747-238Bs from Qantas, one of which was painted, but the deal fell through before the planes left Sydney.

National Airlines bought two, based in Miami and sporting their modish new two-tone cheatline and Sun God on the tail in pineapple-themed yellow and red. This was a decent effort for a fairly small carrier, and the pair of 747s, delivered in September and October 1970, were flown up the east coast to New York, and on the

▲ The Flying Tiger Line was started in 1945 by US war veterans as a classic fly-by-night cargo, trooping and passenger charter outfit, and grew into a global freight giant operating 34 747 Classics, both dedicated freighters and passenger conversions such as this ex-American Airlines 747-123. Flying Tigers was bought by Federal Express for a billion dollars in 1989, turning FedEx from a US-only to a worldwide brand name overnight.

▲ Ten window upper deck but actually a 747-100, originally delivered to Japan Airlines in December 1972

airline's new nonstop from the Sunshine State out to the Golden State, Miami to Los Angeles.

Although surviving the 1973 oil crisis which saw the price of fuel quadruple overnight, by 1976, in a fairly sluggish economy, the 747s were just too much aeroplane for National's short and medium haul network, and the airline standardised on the DC-10. The pair of 747s, Patricia and Linda, spent their whole lives together, going to Northwest Orient in April 1976 and flying there until retirement, when they were parted out side-by-side at Greenwood, Mississippi in early 1994.

Braniff started out as a conservative Texas-based regional carrier that expanded to touch both coasts and, with the installation of ex Continental Airlines vice president Harding Lawrence as CEO, became world famous for a very distinctive fashion sense and a corporate branding that stood out from the crowd, such as their 'jelly bean' fuselages – each aircraft was painted a different colour. Innovative Boeing route planners helped make the case that a market existed for Braniff to deploy a single 747 on a new flight, operating a daily rotation out of Dallas to Honolulu in the middle of the Pacific, an eight-hour trip each way. With the low per-seat costs of a jumbo, the route thrived after N601BN, the one-hundredth 747, was delivered in its famous Big Orange livery on January 5, 1971.

Alas, at the end of the seventies, when the US domestic market was deregulated, Braniff went on an expansion spree that quickly overcame the company's means; before the May 12, 1982 bankruptcy and shutdown, one 747-227B and three 747SP-27s were added to the original Big Orange, alongside leased 747s from Lufthansa, American and CP Air. Two more factory-fresh 747-227Bs were built not delivered, and went instead to Northwest Orient, in a similar fashion to Patricia and Linda.

Continental struggled to find places to fly their first four 747-124s and sold them to Iran in 1975. 1980s low cost pioneer PEOPLExpress weren't nearly as shy, but the burden of running seven ex-Qantas 747-238Bs and an ex-Alitalia -243B soon overwhelmed their ability to stay afloat. Continental took over PEOPLExpress at

▲   NASA converted an ex-American Airlines 747-100 to a Shuttle Carrier Aircraft (SCA), initially used to check the aerodynamics of the design of the United States' new space programme by launching Enterprise, a non-spaceflight rated prototype from its back, which would then glide to a safe landing, gaining valuable data about re-entry from orbit. Once the Space Shuttle was in service, the SCA's main function was to fly shuttles freshly returned from space back to Florida for maintenance and turnaround before their next missions. The most adventurous trip for an SCA was to take Enterprise on a goodwill tour in May 1983 to introduce the new kid on the block, stopping over at RAF Fairford (United Kingdom), the West German capital of Cologne/Bonn, the Paris Air Show, Rome, London Stansted and Ottawa. Carrying a shuttle, the SCA was limited to 250 knots and 15,000 feet, which necessitated two refuelling stops for the Atlantic crossing, in Gander (Canada) and Keflavik (Iceland). The first SCA retained its American Airlines cheatline until the 1980s, when the fleet expanded to two machines with the addition of an ex-Japan Airlines 747SR-46, and a formal livery was created with a clean white fuselage and navy blue cheatline.

(NASA)

the beginning of 1987 and had a much more positive second act with the jumbo, flying them on transatlantic routes from their own hub, Houston, and the Newark hub inherited from PEOPLExpress, to London Gatwick and Frankfurt, cross-country to LA, and to Honolulu and Guam. The jumbos were stood down at the turn of the century in favour of Boeing 777-224ERs.

United Airlines, who in the 1970s were a purely US-only domestic carrier, placed an impressive initial order for 18 ships, only seven less than Pan Am, flying hourly on the big trunk routes across the United States, New York to Los Angeles and to San Francisco. Additionally United was the market leader to Hawaii. Peak hour scheduled on domestic mega routes such as Chicago to Los Angeles also got the jumbo treatment. United 747s were unique among the US trunk lines by staying with their original owner for their entire careers. In the 1980s they bought seven 747-238Bs from Qantas and five -123s from American, as well as a pair of factory-fresh 747-222Bs to their own specification.

In 1985 United bought Pan Am's Pacific network in 1985 for $750 million (which in 2020 money would equate to $1.8 billion), followed by Pan Am's Heathrow landing slots. United was an international airline at last and the -100s and -200s (and 11 of Pan Am's old SP-21s, retained for the following decade) were gradually superseded by 32 747-422s, which were retired in November 2017. United will always be remembered as one of the great 747 operators of all time.

American Airlines, also a purely domestic carrier in those days, ordered ten passenger and eight freighter 747s from Boeing, with deliveries beginning in mid-1970. The 747 Luxury Liners were mostly deployed on trunk routes like New York to Los Angeles and Chicago to Los Angeles, plus a starring role for N9675 in hit disaster movie Airport 1975.

The first Delta Air Lines 747-132, N9896, was delivered on September 26, 1970, followed by four more over the following months. Even in a highly regulated market, Delta had beefed up routes and

▲ The 500th 747 delivered was a -283B for SAS

(Boeing)

▲ This faithful machine served its whole life with the Pakistani flag carrier, July 1979 until November 2011

schedules in and out of its Atlanta base sufficiently to operate a thriving hub for transit traffic before the hub-and-spoke concept really existed; despite that commercial advantage, Delta found that, with the 747, in a predictable pattern, had more aeroplane on its hands than it needed. Passengers loved the roomy half-empty 747s from Atlanta to New York or Los Angeles, but the operation was haemorrhaging money, and Delta was soon looking for a buyer. One 747 went to China Airlines of Taiwan and the other three went to Flying Tigers, becoming N803FT, N804FT and N805FT.

The -100 had a bit of life left in it. In September 1977, Boeing announced a new 747 variant known as the -100B, with a reinforced structure and uprated engines but retaining the original lighter structure. Iran Air and Saudia both placed orders, although due to the Iranian Revolution in 1979 and worsening of relations with its erstwhile ally the USA, only the first of four ordered by Iran Air was built. Saudia's eight were the only Rolls-Royce powered 747-100s. 28 additional -100s were built for the domestic market in Japan, known as the 747SR, for short range.

A total of 167 747-100s were delivered to airlines worldwide. As well as those detailed above, early 747 operators included Alitalia, Aer Lingus, Air France, Iberia, Air Canada, and Sabena.

The 747-200B

As early as 1967, an upgraded 747 was under consideration. Modifications to the baseline design were thorough – tougher landing gear, new flap actuators, thicker wing skin, stronger spars, and other structural enhancements. More powerful JT9Ds were coming online as Pratt & Whitney got to grips with the huge turbofan engine they had created, and meanwhile both General Electric and Rolls-Royce were coming up with competing powerplants, the CF6 (which would also power the McDonnell Douglas DC-10 and Airbus A300 / A310) and RB.211 (which would also power the Lockheed L-1011 Tristar and some Boeing 767s) - both

▲ In February 1988 British Airways received its last 747-200B, which was converted to a freighter by Air Atlanta Icelandic in 2001 and leased to other airlines, including the cargo division of Malaysia Airlines

of which were offered to customers for the new 747B, later renamed the 747-200B.

The first 747-200B was built for Northwest Orient, and was the eighty-eighth jumbo to be rolled out of Boeing's Everett plant on September 30, 1970. N611US took to the air for the first time on October 11 and headed down to Edwards AFB in Mojave, California, for flight testing, which included setting a new world record for maximum take off weight: 820,700 pounds (372,263 kilograms), beating the previous record set by a USAF Lockheed C-5A by ten tonnes. The first 747-200B in service was KLM's PH-BUA Mississippi in February 1971; Northwest received N611US from Boeing the following month.

The initial 747-200Bs were fitted with the classic three windows in the upper deck but the increased maximum takeoff weight of the -200B allowed for more payload and the upper deck was internally stretched by 1.9 metres (six feet) to 7.62 metres (26 feet) so ten windows on the upper deck became the norm. The increased space allowed room for conventional airline seating upstairs, usually in four rows of recliners to make a business class cabin of 16, quite a windfall for the accountants; the days of the cocktail lounge were now numbered. The first 747-200B with the internally stretched upper deck and ten windows was Qantas' first jumbo, VH-EBA City Of Canberra, delivered in July 1971. This was also the first Boeing widebody with a galley in the belly, reached by a lift from the main deck.

The 747-200B, with its enhanced capabilities driven by structural improvements, engines that had come of age at last, is probably the truest symbol of the great human migration that began with air transport. Not only was oil a mere three dollars a barrel ($17 dollars in 2020 money) but perhaps more importantly, didn't fluctuate more than a few cents either side of three bucks all the way from 1948 to 1973. Accountants like a bargain, but they love certainty. This incredible run of free energy and economic continuity for an industry that relies on both for its existence drove the mass migration of humanity more than any other factor. The 747 was incredibly efficient compared to the narrowbody airliners of the 1960s, and represented an epic, revolutionary change in productivity for airlines.

And hey, if the incredibly low price of energy meant there was a bit of room for extras like the upper deck cocktail lounge, or nine abreast seating in economy which would easily compete in both seat width and legroom of today's premium economy products (and handily beat them with the high quality and quantity of food and service), why not? It hadn't yet occurred to the industry that it was possible to do air travel without that kind of style and comfort, although ironically it was the 747 that demonstrated to the airlines how much money they could make with economies of scale.

Some countries had a sole 747 as a flagship with a lot of national pride riding onboard, such as Air Gabon, Air Madagascar, Cameroon Airlines, providing a vital diplomatic and trade bridge with the world.

Other airlines couldn't get enough, especially in Asia. Japan Airlines operated nearly 50 747-100s and -200s (including a dozen freighters); All Nippon Airways (ANA), who in those days had no international traffic rights outside Japan at all, was still able to deploy 17 747s just on domestic routes. The Japanese Domestic 747, known as the 747SR (Short Range) or 747D (Domestic) was a special variant beefed up for high-cycle flying (a cycle is a flight – take off and landing). Structure, landing gear, brakes and other elements were all heavier.

A couple of European airlines really stand out for taking on board this American import and absolutely thriving – most notably, British Airways had 19 -136s and 23 -236Bs, and Lufthansa five -130s and 22 -230Bs (12 with main deck side cargo doors). These fleets flew to six continents on a daily basis, a huge triumph for the operators and for the financial well-being of their home countries, and, for that matter, that of the countries they flew to.

Almost every 747 carrier in Europe flew to Australia, a 10,000 mile (16,000 km) trip – British Airways, UTA, Lufthansa, Alitalia, Olympic Airways tail fins all lined up at Sydney and Melbourne on a semi-daily basis. In the 1970s and 1980s, the Persian Gulf, today site of the biggest airline hubs the world has ever seen (Emirates' A380 order of 140 ships is nearly as much as the entire production run of the 747-100) was a sleepy tech stop for a few jumbos dropping in for fuel in the middle of the night such as Qantas QF1 to London, or Cathay Pacific's early forays into Europe from Hong Kong.

Three unique 747-2B4B(SCD)s were delivered to Lebanon's national carrier Middle East Airlines (MEA) in 1975 just as the country descended into a brutal civil war that lasted 15 years. Their main deck side cargo door (hence SCD) made them highly flexible, able to fly passengers, cargo, or a combination of both, and hence commanded high lease rates for MEA, who used the hard currency earnings to meet their payroll during the conflict. Their 747s served in the liveries of Gulf Air, Egyptair, Saudia, Nigeria Airways, Air France, Garuda and British Airways among others, often in pairs. With the war in Lebanon finally over at the end of 1990, they were returned to MEA service and spent the 1990s finally connecting Beirut to the world, 15 years later than intended.

Boeing sold 393 747-200s, which breaks down as 225 passenger -200Bs, 78 747-200M combis, 73 -200F pure freighters, and 13 747-200C convertible freighters. Today there is only a tiny handful of 747-200 freighters out there, and all passenger aircraft have been retired.

The 747SP

The genesis of the 747SP was Pan Am and Iran Air's joint 1973 request to Boeing for a new 747 that would be able to cover greater distance than the -200B. Pan Am wanted to fly the polar route from New York to Tokyo without having to stop in Anchorage for fuel en route, and California to Sydney without the stop in Honolulu. Iran Air's flagship route from Tehran to New York was stopping in London in both directions for a top up and the ambitious carrier wanted to go nonstop. Boeing were also aware of the large capacity gap between the 707 and the 747 which was being eagerly filled by the three-engined McDonnell Douglas DC-10

▲ The 747SP was vital for South Africa in the days of apartheid and they were denied overflight rights by most African nations, the circuitous route greatly lengthening the flight time to Europe

and Lockheed L-1011, a market they could join with a smaller 747 variant.

The internal decision to proceed with what was initially known as the 747SB – Short Body – was made in June 1973, and publicly announced as the 747SP – Special Performance – on 23 August of the same year, with orders from Pan Am and Iran Air. The baseline design was the 747-100, and the specifications for its little sister revolved around a shrink of 48 feet and four inches (14.7 metres) less fuselage length.

The other visible differences were in the empennage – due to the shorter moment arm from the centre of the aircraft to its extremities, the stabilisers, both horizontal (also known as the tailplane) and vertical (also known as the fin, or just, the tail) had to be extended to exact the same control authority. While the horizontal stabiliser's extra ten feet (three metres) of span was not noticeable except perhaps to a flight engineer looking up during his preflight walk-around inspection, the vertical stabiliser's extra five feet (1.5 metres) was obvious. The rudder was the same size as on the 747-200 but doubled-hinged to increase control authority.

To make the 747SP fly as much like the 747 Classic as possible, Boeing included test pilots in the design programme who logged hundreds of hours in a new state-of-the-art simulator which duplicated the responses of the both the Classic and the SP in all flight regimes. Boeing used the feedback to tailor the flight control system as well as autothrottle, speedbrakes, flaps, landing gear, wheel brakes, nose-wheel steering and thrust reversers. Pilots from potential customer airlines also took part.

Production took place on a separate line within the 200-million square foot (18.6 million square metres) 747 plant at Everett, used in the early days of the 747 programme to fulfil the huge initial demand for the new jumbo, and had since closed.

The first 747SP to fly was N747SP (later N530PA with Pan Am) in a patriotic red-white-and-blue livery, taking off from Paine Field, Everett, on US Independence Day, 4 July 1975, for a sortie lasting three hours and four minutes under the command of Jack Waddell. The aircraft was put through its paces, flown at speeds of up to Mach 0.92 and slow enough to be fully stalled; and up as high as 30,000 feet. Later in the day, another 52 minute flight ferried the aircraft across to Boeing Field in Seattle where the test programme would continue.

The 747SP's first flight in passenger service was on April 25, 1976 from Los Angeles to Tokyo. The next day inaugurated the route the SP was intended for, PA800 from New York JFK to Tokyo nonstop. As Pan Am received the next three 747SPs built, service was extended to Europe, South America and nonstop from New York to Bahrain.

Iran Air was the second airline to receive the 747SP, starting with EP-IAA in a ceremony at Boeing Field on March 12, 1976, where the aircraft remained for the next month for the training of 16 Iranian pilots and eight flight engineers, as the SP was Iran Air's first 747 of any kind. Service commenced in mid-June on the prestigious New York run. Due to Tehran Mehrabad's high altitude and high temperatures, plus en-route headwinds, the westbound service still routed through London Heathrow, but the eastbound flight covered the 6,296 miles (10,132 kilometres) nonstop.

South African Airways' first 747SP delivery was nonstop from Everett to Cape Town, a staggering 10,290 miles (16,560 kilometres), flown in 17 hours and 22 minutes. Scheduled service commenced on May 1, flying Johannesburg-Athens-Rome-Lisbon. Two more aircraft were soon delivered, and, on August 1, replaced the 707 on flights to New York, with a refueling stop on Sal Island in the Atlantic Ocean, shaving two hours off the old routing via Rio.

Other airline customers for the SP were Qantas, Saudia, Syrianair, China Airlines of Taiwan, Braniff International, Air China, Korean Air, Royal Air Maroc and TWA. Secondhand operators included Aerolineas Argentinas, Tajik Air, and Luxair. American Airlines bought TWA's planes to open their first flight to Japan, Dallas to Tokyo nonstop.

However, most airlines wouldn't take the bait, and final sales efforts resulted in just one more order for a standard 747SP, for the Royal Flight of Bahrain, taking to the air on March 31 1987, five years after the second-last 747SP was delivered (to the Iraqi government), and delivered on September 12, 1989 after a 30-month fitting out. Only 45 747SPs were built.

Iran Air, marooned with their all-Boeing fleet after the Iranian Revolution of 1979 but no way to buy more planes due to a major falling-out with the United States, kept their pre-revolutionary 747SP fleet in the air until 2014, when EP-IAC ran out of hours and flew its last service from Bombay home to Tehran on June 11 then ferried from Khomeini International (IKA) to the airline's maintenance base at Mehrabad (THR) where she and her three sisters reside to this day.

Today, because the 747SP is still such a hot rod, out of the 45 built, ten are still in service as VIP transports for various governments, mostly in the Middle East, or providing an invite-only luxury shuttle between Las Vegas and Macau for high rolling gambling on behalf of Sands Casinos.

The 747-300

Boeing had been looking at stretching the 747 throughout the 1970s, and at the beginning of the 1980s launched the 747-300 with an order from Swissair. The main body of the plane was not stretched, and internal systems were not meaningfully updated, but the upper deck now reached back to end above the wings, adding 23 feet and four inches (7.11 metres) to the upper deck's external dimensions.

The -300 first flew on October 5, 1982, and Swissair received their first machine on March 23, 1983, followed by French long haul pioneer UTA (Union de Transports Aeriens), Air-India, Qantas, Saudia, Cathay Pacific, Japan Airlines, KLM, Varig, Singapore Airlines, South African and Thai International. Additionally, KLM modified eight of its -200Bs with a retrofitted upper deck stretch to match its new -300s; UTA and Japan Airlines did the same with two each.

In the secondhand market, the 747-300 flew on, with Pakistan International Airlines (PIA) buying six from Cathay Pacific, adding another blue chip name to 747-300 operators, and Air France inheriting three 747-3B3s when they took over UTA. The latter were later sold on to Iranian giant Mahan Air where one still flies today (with old-fashioned 'Treasure Island' style maps of the French Caribbean islands still intact on their cabin dividers). TAAG Angola operated two ships (one ex-Swissair, one ex-Singapore Airlines) out of their Luanda base to two of the world's major lusaphone cities: up to Lisbon, and across the South Atlantic to Sao Paolo. Ansett Australia picked up a pair from Singapore Airlines which they flew out of Sydney to Hong Kong, Osaka, Seoul, Shanghai, Taipei and Kuala Lumpur until their 2001 bankruptcy.

Although there were no 747-300 freighters built, the stretched upper deck actually helped with the aerodynamics of the design, and there were some slight tweaks to the wing compared to the -200B, so whatever the added weight of the -300 extra structure was, it was more than countered by these enhancements, and so 20 -300s were converted to have a second life as freighters, known as the 747-300BCF (Boeing Converted Freighter).

Since the airlines were somewhat aware that a sea-change was coming to the 747, none of them went in for huge orders and most preferred to wait altogether – indeed the 747-300 was never ordered by any North American carrier, and other perennial operators such as British Airways and Lufthansa also held out. Nonetheless it is impressive that 81 -300s were built, including 21 -300M combis with main deck side cargo doors, and four -300D domestic models for the Japanese market. The last two 747-300s were delivered to Sabena in 1990, and these were 747-300-and-a-half aircraft, with aerodynamic refinements that can be seen on the -300's successor, especially around the wing-body join.

Boeing announced the 747-300A (for Advanced) at the Farnborough Airshow in September 1984. Like the -300s rolling off the line in Seattle, the -300A was a 'minimum change' upgrade, still incorporating a three-person analogue cockpit and little else in the way of innovation.

In early 1985, British Airways, Cathay Pacific, Qantas, Singapore Airlines, KLM, Lufthansa and Northwest Airlines assembled a consultative group to compare notes on common requirements for a truly new 747 and to join forces to lobby Boeing to make something a bit more magical happen, to make use of

▲ The 747 evolves into the -300; the upper deck is stretched, but still no winglets

the leaps forward made in metallurgy, construction, and especially digital avionics, as demonstrated by the two-person cockpits of the Boeing 757 and 767 that had debuted in the early 1980s and were light years ahead of the steam gauges found in the cockpit of the 747-300. Northwest was first to put their hat into the ring with an order for ten of the new variant, announced on October 22, 1985, jumpstarting the next chapter in the story of the 747.

The -400 Emerges

After three years of design and construction, the new variant was dubbed the 747-400. From that moment, the previous variants, the -100, -200B, SP and -300 were known as 747 Classics.

The first 747-400, N401PW, was rolled out of the hangar at Everett on January 26, 1988 (and in a coup for Boeing, the first 737-400 was rolled out at nearby Renton on the same day). The registration suffix was a tip of the hat to the new Pratt & Whitney PW4056 engines, the first of three engine options available to customers.

Under the skin were extra fuel tanks in the horizontal stabiliser with room for 3,000 gallons (12,000 litres), bigger wheels, hi-tech carbon brakes, restyled cabin architecture, a new APU (auxiliary power unit) from Pratt & Whitney Canada, and a totally new two-person digital cockpit, which reduced the 971 knobs, dials, switches and gauges found in the front office of the Classic to a very user-friendly 365.

The upgrades in the 747-400 were recognisable even to the relatively untrained eye. As well as retaining the stretched upper deck of the -300, the wingspan was increased by 17 feet (5.2 metres) and sprouted six foot (1.8 metre) winglets which alone improved fuel burn by two percent by taming the wing tip vortices. Despite the extra structure, the new wings were 6,000 lbs (2,700 kilograms) lighter.

The 747-400's first flight took place on April 29, 1988, piloted by James Loesch and Kenneth Higgins, and lasted two hours and 26 minutes. Having departed

▲ Eva Air blasting out of LAX, destination Taipei, exactly the kind of long haul the 747-400 was intended for
◄ The prototype 747-400 is joined in the skies over Seattle by the original 747 prototype (Boeing)

from Paine Field at Everett, the flight landed at Boeing Field just south of downtown Seattle where the test programme began.

The second 747-400 to fly was N5573S, powered by General Electric CF6-80 engines and was destined to become D-ABVB at Lufthansa; the third, N1788B, was powered by Rolls-Royce RB211-535Gs, and became Cathay Pacific's VR-HOO. A fourth, also powered with PW4062s, was registered N662US and destined for Northwest, used as a 'hot spare' back-up.

During testing, one of the machines set the record for the world's heaviest plane by getting airborne at a weight of 892,450 pounds (401,810 kilograms). The test programme was an indicator of the success the new Boeing flagship would have in service, proceeding without incident in all flight regimes. The Pratt & Whitney-powered 747-400 was certified in the USA by the FAA on January 9, 1989, and N401PW, having been reregistered N661US and reconfigured to the specs of Northwest Airlines, was prepared for its inaugural revenue flight, which took place on February 9 on a short hop from the airline's snowy hub at Minneapolis down to the desert city of Phoenix.

The 747-400 Into Service

Singapore Airlines was the second airline to take delivery of a 747-400 and were the first to operate an international flight, putting their new flagship, branded MegaTop in service (the -300 was the BigTop), on the long haul to London on May 31, 1989. Northwest, having kept the aircraft on domestic runs for crew training, opened their own long haul service with the new type the next day on June 1, from New York to Tokyo.

European certification by the Joint Aviation Authorities (JAA) hit an unexpected hurdle, as it was felt that the aircraft would not meet their newly-implemented and more demanding requirements for withstanding serious structural damage, specifically the floor of the upper deck, which was determined to not be able to survive a sudden decompression caused by a 20 foot (6.1 metre) square hole without potentially catastrophic damage to control cables and wiring.

A 90-day temporary certificate was granted to allow KLM to take delivery on May 18 and Lufthansa on May 23, and Boeing agreed to produce retrofit kits to strengthen their floor beams and separate control runs. Subsequent 747-400s emerged from the factory built to the improved standard. British Airways, the first airline to operate the Rolls-Royce powered -400 received their first aircraft, G-BNLA, on June 30.

Qantas, another loyal Rolls-Royce customer, made headlines with the delivery flight of their first 747-400, VH-OJA City Of Canberra, which ferried from Seattle to London and, leaving on August 17, was flown nonstop from London to Sydney in 20 hours and nine minutes, setting a distance and endurance record for a jet airliner.

The 747-400 dominated the long haul airways of the 1990s and 2000s as the biggest and most prestigious airliner in the sky. Major customers included Singapore Airlines with 42, United Airlines and Lufthansa with 28 each, Qantas with 25, Air France with 23.

The size, safety and prestige of the 747-400 meant that 11 fly even now as head of state VIP transports, including one in full Air China livery for the Beijing government. Japan's Self Defence Force acquired two (now in the final stages of retirement, to be replaced by 777-300ERs), based at Sapporo in northern Japan. South Korea has a head of state 747-400 based at Seoul Kimpo. The Sultan of Brunei flies his own 747-400 as pilot in command. The rest are all based in the Persian Gulf, with one in the service of the Bahrein Royal Flight, one in a special Kingdom of Saudi Arabia livery as well as a Saudi Royal Flight aircraft in the colours of the national airline, two at the Dubai Air Wing, and one at the other big city of the United Arab Emirates — the Abu Dhabi Amiri Flight. In addition, General Electric operate a 747-400 as a flying test bed for new aeroengines, and Virgin Galactic have converted one into a satellite launcher.

As they had with the -100 and -200, Boeing developed a sub-type for the demanding Japanese domestic market, where so many passengers fly between cities that widebody aircraft are the standard. The -400D, successor to the -100SR and -300SR, was

▲ Japan Airlines (JAL) was the biggest 747 operator with over 100 747s in their fleet flying at one time

▲ Japan's head of state transport wing is based in Sapporo, and keep their skills sharp by flying training flights between missions, here in formation with a pair of locally-built Mitsubishi F-15J fighter jets

▲ Air New Zealand's main 747 route was to London via Los Angeles, two very long sectors back-to-back. This bird is blasting out of Los Angeles, but is she heading home or away?

▲ Philippines used their 747s both for range, such as to Vancouver and Los Angeles, and for pure people moving, as RP-C7473 comes in to land at the end of the short flight to Hong Kong

▲ Delta out of LAX and Malaysia out of Sydney at the start of transpacific crossings

sold to both All Nippon Airways, who took 13 alongside 14 regular -400s, and Japan Airlines who took nine alongside a whopping 40 of the regular -400. The -400D was most visibly recognisable for its lack of winglets, which only produce real savings in cruise. Since most domestic sectors in Japan clock in at under an hour, their weight undermined any saving in fuel burn. The wingtips were optimised for the addition of winglets, although conversion to long haul operations happened to only four -400Ds in practice.

During the Japanese economic boom of the 1990s, some of Japan Airlines' 40 mainline -400s had a seating configuration for just 303 passengers, including 91 in business class; United Airlines went even further, with a special layout for some Pacific routes that seated 36 in first and a bottom-line (and bottom pleasing) 123 in business, leaving room for only 15 rows of economy class accommodating 142, bringing the total to just 301.

These ended with the coming of a recession to Japan, but the most luxurious passenger 747 still flies — Atlas Air's three passenger 747-400s are operated on behalf of Angolan oil specialist Sonair on its three-times-a-week 15 hour nonstop service from Luanda to Houston, with a layout of ten first, 143 business and 36 economy.

British Airways expanded their 747-436 fleet until it reached 57 aircraft, flying twice daily all the way to Sydney, twice daily to Tokyo, Miami, San Francisco, and adding frequency on the run to New York almost without limit. The fleet passed through three liveries, starting with the Landor scheme, taking on over a dozen identities in the unpopular but colourful Utopia scheme, before settling on the current Chatham Historic Dockyard colours that was developed in the Utopia era for Concorde alone and hurriedly adopted fleetwide.

British Airways requested a unique variant, known as the 747 Lite. Aboard G-CIVF, 'VG, 'VH, and 'VI, the 12,490 litre fuel tank in the vertical stabiliser was not plumbed in, enabling a recertification with a lower maximum takeoff weight from 875,015 lbs (396,900 kilograms) to 839,961 lbs (381,000 kilograms), increasing payload by 13,228 lbs (6,000 kilograms) and still paying lower landing fees and overflight fees (albeit by sacrificing some range). The only visible difference is found in the cockpit, where two fuel tank switches are replaced by a blank panel.

The Jumbo Evolves Again

As early as the 1990s Boeing began looking at a stretched 747 variant. The 1996 Farnborough Airshow was where these plans were first seen in public, with the proposed 747-500X and -600X, two different fuselage lengths with a 777 wing. Although generating much curiosity and fanfare around the world even in the mainstream press due to the global fame and prestige of the 'jumbo jet', airlines were not persuaded to make a purchase. By the turn of the century, Airbus were gearing up with the A380 double decker (in those years known as the A3XX), and Boeing stepped back into the fray. With a new and wider wing, the 747X had the same fuselage and capacity of a 747-400, and the 747X Stretch would be ten metres (32 feet nine inches) longer.

Although the 747X designations didn't make it to the production line, plenty of design elements were appropriated to create a somewhat underappreciated step in the jumbo's evolutionary process, the 747-400ER and 747-400ERF. The passenger variant was announced with an order by Qantas for six 747-400ERs, to fly nonstop from Melbourne to Los Angeles in both directions without a payload penalty. This 747X is also known as the 910 because of its increased maximum take off weight of 910,000 pounds (412,775 kilograms), 35,000 pounds (15,885 kilograms) more than a -400, which could be used either for extra payload over a regular distance, or to carry extra fuel to extract an extra 500 miles (805 kilometres) of range. The Qantas 747-438ERs, the only passenger ERs, are recognisable by their General Electric CF6s in place of the fully-ducted Rolls-Royce Trents on common-or-garden Qantas 747-400s.

Qantas was the only passenger airline that really needed the extra performance, but cargo airlines, much more weight-driven, were eager for the enhancements to become available and thus Boeing were able to deliver

▲ The prototype 747-8i in flight over the Cascade Mountains in Washington State (Boeing)

40 747-400ERF freighters, starting with Air France on October 17, 2002 and ending with the last delivery of any -400, to Kalitta Air on December 22, 2009.

In the midst of that period, orders for passenger 747s dried up under the twin onslaught of the big twin 777 and the double deck A380. The last 747-400 passenger liner was B-18215 delivered to China Airlines of Taiwan on April 26, 2005.

Boeing were faced with making a leap into the unknown or getting out of the 747 business altogether. The engineering division had a catch-all paper aeroplane called the 747 Advanced where the best elements of the proposed jumbos was incorporated, such as a fuselage stretch, raked wingtips and a saw-tooth trailing edge for the engine nacelle. On November 14, Boeing made the leap and announced the 747 Advanced was now the Boeing 747-8.

The 747-8i

Other than 45 747SPs built in the 1970s and early 1980s, the length of the 747 had never been altered. The 747-8 was stretched by 18 feet and four inches (5.6 metres) and the new wingspan is 13 feet and one inch (four metres) wider than the 747-400. Production of the first airframes – initially freighters – began at Everett at the beginning of August 2008. Even in its new form, the passenger variant was proving to be a tough sell, especially as Boeing were short of engineering resources and suffered from unexpected design changes and other shortfalls as the year went on.

At the start of 2009, with only one order for passenger aircraft in the bag, Boeing announced publicly that it was "reassessing" the 747-8, as more production delays pushed the first flight into 2010. But Cargolux were just as positive they wanted their 13 aircraft, and Lufthansa reaffirmed their commitment

▲ Lufthansa, a 747 operator from the start, was the launch customer for the 747-8i

to the programme by confirming their order for 19 passenger 747-8i (Intercontinental) passenger aircraft.

The programme picked up morale at the end of 2009 with successful engine runs and an order from Korean Air for ten 747-8is. On February 8, 2010, N747EX, the first 747-8F took to the skies on its maiden flight, lasting three hours and 37 minutes over Washington State. After local test flights out of Moses Lake, N747EX ferried to Palmdale in the California desert, to be clear of the 787 which was working through a troubled test programme of its own at nearby Boeing Field. The second 747-8 got airborne on March 15 followed by the third just two days later. With the 747-400s all delivered and the -8 yet to begin production, 2010 was the only year since 1969 in which Boeing delivered zero 747s.

August 21 saw a 747 smash yet another record, when N747EX got airborne weighing 1,005,000 pounds (455,860 kilograms), the first time any flying machine had lifted off heavier than a million pounds in weight. This was an instructive moment – even 40 years into its life, the 747 was still at the cutting edge of what was possible.

The test programme revealed some issues that required design changes, most notably the main landing gear doors had to be reshaped as they caused buffeting – the third test aircraft was dedicated to solving this issue. A weakness was identified in structural longerons in the upper fuselage which was fixed by using a more robust manufacturing process, but the cause of structural oscillation and aileron flutter were harder to diagnose. First deliveries were postponed to early 2011, when a fifth 747-8F joined the programme on February 3, followed by the first 747-8i on March 20 and a second 747-8i on April 26.

The first 747-8F was handed over in a lavish ceremony to launch customer Cargolux at Everett on October 12 to start piloting training, and the FAA awarded type certification on December 14, 2011, after which Cargolux placed the aircraft into revenue service.

The first 747-8i was delivered to Lufthansa on May 5, 2012, and entered service on the daily schedule from Frankfurt to Washington Dulles. Cargo airlines did buy the jet, but not in huge numbers – the 747-8 ramp-up coincided with a sluggish global economy so up to the present time, total orders stand at 154: 41 747-8i passenger aircraft (with no further orders on the horizon, regrettably) and 113 747-8F freighters.

The Queen Of The Skies

At the end of 2015 a production cut to half an aeroplane per month (six per year) was announced, to keep the line open long enough to build two new Air Force One presidential airliners to replace the 747-200s used by every president since George H. W. Bush in the early 1990s.

Just in time, US parcel giant UPS came in for an order for 14 747-8Fs at the end of 2016. This was exactly the kind of order that Boeing had been holding out for – an established 747 operator's existing fleet of 747-400s was ageing out to the point of needing replacement. There are around 200 747-400 freighters flying today, and for some missions there is nothing else that will take its place – with the high payload weights in the freight hauling business, the extra engines really pay their way compared to a widebody twin.

The advent of the Covid-19 novel coronavirus in early 2020 has resulted in an almost complete grounding of passenger airlines, with the recovery expected to be slow. Qantas, KLM and other 747 operators who expected to fly their last -400s for one or two more years announced that these fleets would not return to service, heartbreaking for these old birds who did so much for the countries and the people they flew for, and deserved a more dignified end. Half of all air cargo flies in the bellies of passenger airliners, so with reduced passenger flying, the downtown may actually drive the need for more dedicated freighters. That said, at the time of writing, Boeing are telegraphing a 2022 shut down for the 747 line. So while the end is in sight, there is still a chance of a few top up 747-8F orders

So hopefully there will be more orders like the UPS windfall, and with the fiftieth anniversary of 747 deliveries to airlines marked last year, the Queen Of The Skies has celebrated a golden jubilee which no other widebody jet can touch, and still plays a vital role in global commerce. This is the jet that taught the whole world to fly.

▲ Thai International pay tribute to the history of aviation with this special 747 retrojet

Korean Air 747-400 And -8i

Korean Air have been in the 747 club since the mid-1970s, when they received 747-200Bs factory-fresh from Boeing, followed by some second hand examples from Lufthansa, a pair of extra long range SPs to operate the polar route from Seoul to New York nonstop, and a pair of -300s in the mid 80s as South Korea's economy embraced democracy after decades of autocratic dictatorship, and began its impressive trajectory towards today's industrial and cultural powerhouse, where it is the twelfth biggest economy in the world.

The 747-400 arrived just in time, and Korean Air (previously Korean Air Lines; the rebrand was a response to a series of disastrous accidents, which also included tightening up cockpit procedures, making

today's airline one of the world's safest) operated 25 passenger models, and over 30 freighters. Korean Air is such a big fan of the 747 that they are one of the select trio of airlines who fly the 747-8i passenger variant, with a fleet of ten alongside seven 747-8F freighters.

I managed to fly two sectors on the 747-400 in the last years of the type's career at Korean Air, when the Queen of the Skies had already been dislodged from the flagship long haul routes to Europe, North America, and Australia by the more efficient 777-300ER, but still paying her way on local flights to Japan, China, Singapore, Vietnam, Thailand and Guam.

My first leg was from Hong Kong to Seoul/Incheon. The common-use SkyTeam lounge at Hong Kong is located beneath the departures level, with only a few windows and they were in any case covered with blinds, creating the sensation of being underground. Food offering was generous with a noodle bar and a special, Hong Kong fish shomai. Seating was ample. ▶

▲ Intercontinental first class on the 747-400 with an attractive choice of colours and screen placement

▲ A stunning array of savoury meal options in Korean Air first class, even on an intra-Asian hop, including the famous bibimbap, bottom right

▲ Some of Korean Air's 747-400s have a regional first class hard product

I was thrilled to see HL7472 waiting at the gate. Onboard, I was shown to my first class seat in the nose of the jumbo, and kind and friendly cabin crew offered me Perrier Jouet champagne as a predeparture beverage. We blasted off runway 7R at the beginning of our three hour flight to Korea, the land of morning calm. The 'light meal' was seven delicious courses, including a bibimbap, Korea's most famous dish. All washed down with champagne and green tea!

After a night in Seoul, my plan was to continue my journey to Singapore aboard the new flagship, the 747-8i. Alas, at check-in I discovered that my ship was in the hangar for maintenance, and another 747-400 had been drafted into service. Consolation was that I would be the only passenger in first class this morning. After making my way through security (no fast track for premium passengers), I spent some time relaxing in Korean Air's first class lounge, which, while lacking the wow factor of a Cathay or Qantas lounge, was a solid product, including Bottega Gold champagne, served from a gold bottle.

At the gate, there was a notice posted explaining the ship change from the -8i to the -400 – apparently Korean Air and their passengers take this kind of thing quite seriously! Despite being mocked by the sight of an -8i being towed onto the next door gate for the San Francisco flight, I was still thrilled to be flying on a 747 and turning left upon boarding!

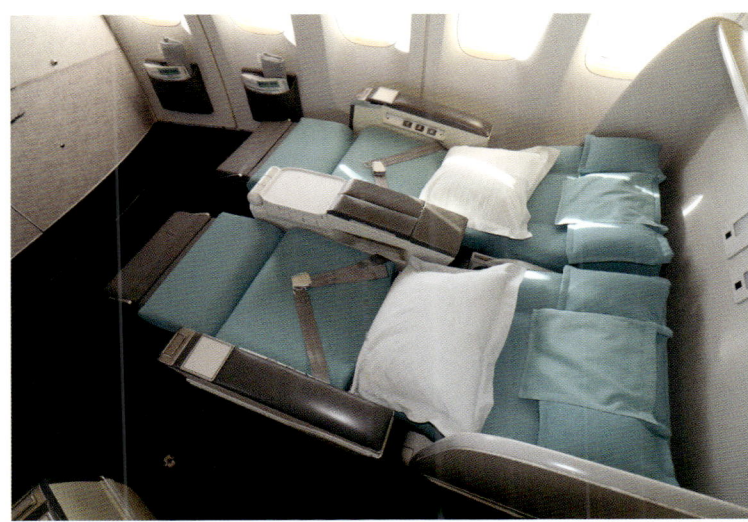

▲ Not quite fully flat, but still very comfortable

▲ Business class on the upper deck of the 747-400

This jumbo had a regional, not intercontinental, first class product. Seats were recliners in pairs as opposed to yesterday's enormous flat bed suite. With a short taxi (but long enough for the flight attendant to be embarrassed by giving the safety demonstration to a single passenger – me), we leapt off runway 33L and set course for Singapore, six hours to the south.

Another delicious six course light meal! After the green tea ice cream finale, I asked the flight attendants to turn all 12 seats into beds for a photo. Then I went to the upper deck, where I was surprised to find only one passenger. When business class is spread between the main deck and the upper deck, it is the upper deck, perceived as more private and more prestigious, that fills up first. Today, for some reason, was the reverse!

I enjoyed a two hour nap back at my seat, and woke to enjoy the sunset over the South China Sea. There were thunderstorms building to one side and I felt the captain manually bank the aeroplane away towards clearer skies. No better place to feel those small adjustments than the nose of the 747. The second meal was served, an enormous portion of steak, noodles, and dessert. I was so full as we descended for a smooth touchdown on runway 22C at Singapore's Changi airport, one of the world's best airports. I had missed out on the 747-8i but Korean Air had delivered a very special experience.

▲ With my book Air2, which featured a Korean Air A380 on the cover

▲ Business class on the upper deck of the 747-8i

One year later, I tried the same route again to score a Korean Air 747-8i, and this time I succeeded!

I booked my trip from Hong Kong to Singapore via Seoul with 45,000 Korean Air Skypass frequent flier points in first class. (SPG Starwood, the frequent guest programme for Sheraton Hotels, are a transfer partner of Skypass and their Star Points can be purchased with cash, making for excellent value redemptions.)

Once again, I was the only passenger travelling first today. Korean Air's current first class product is a very private suite with a door that can slide closed. For privacy I recommend 3A or 3K; 1A and 1K are the closest to each other (as the cabin tapers to the nose) for couples. We took off from runway 07R and I caught a glimpse of Kowloon and even Hong Kong's old Kai Tak airport. Before the meal service began, I took a quick tour of business class on both the main deck and upper deck. Korean Air's newest business class product is one of the best in the sky, flat beds and staggered to give even window seat passengers direct aisle access.

I could barely move after the 'light meal' that would suffice on a 12 hour flight. I enjoyed the beautiful sunset between Taiwan and Korea, and was grateful to have finally flown on Korean Air's new flagship. Korean Air combine modern luxury and tradition, and today are one of the world's top travel brands. I hope to fly them again soon – from the land of morning calm to the world.

▲ First class suites in the nose of the 747-8i

▲ Deep blue late afternoon sunshine as we cruise towards Korea

Iran Air: Classic 747s Over Persia

▲ Boarding EP-IAG on the ramp at IKA for an early morning flight down to Dubai

▲ Homa Class in the nose of the jumbo

▲ A half-empty conomy class, but the return leg will be packed

Both for aviation megafun, and for culture and hospitality, there is nowhere in the world like Iran. Iran in the mid-twentieth century was a booming nation due to its resource wealth and highly educated population. However, years of superpower meddling led to a popular uprising in 1979, deposing the king, Shah Mohammad Reza Pahlevi, in favour of a revolutionary Islamic government led by Ayatollah Khomeini. This led to a worsening of relations with erstwhile ally the United States, leading to sanctions against Iran which made acquiring new aircraft impossible.

The Shah had been very aviation-minded and equipped flag carrier Iran Air with a modern fleet including seven 747s. (In fact Iran Air was the only airline to place a confirmed order for Concordes outside of Britain and France, which were cancelled by the new regime.)

Iran Air's first jumbos were 747SPs, ordered specifically for their long range, to allow nonstop service from New York back to Tehran (nonstop westbound was still out of reach due to Tehran's high altitude – a mile above sea level – which diminished the performance of even the mighty SP, which refueled on the westbound trip to the United States in London Heathrow). These were EP-IAA, AB, AC and AD. The first two were delivered to Tehran in early 1976, followed by a pair of 747-200Bs later the same year, EP-IAG and AH.

The 747-100 was superceded by the -200B in the Boeing sales portfolio, but in the late 1970s they devised an uprated incarnation called the -100B which combined the lighter structure of the -100 with elements of the -200B, to create a subvariant called the -100B. This was intended for Middle East carriers for busy regional routes that required the capacity of the 747 but not necessarily its intercontinental range. Four each were ordered by Saudia and Iran Air. Alas only one of Iran's -100Bs was built – EP-IAM – before the change of regime in Tehran, so AN, AP and AR remained paper aeroplanes.

Iran Air's final 747 addition was a 747-230B originally delivered to Lufthansa in February 1982 and acquired by Iran in March 2008. This bird had one difference with the rest of Iran Air's fleet, which was that

▲ Iran Air is famous for turning their planes into exotic Persian restaurants at meal times

▲ Homa class breakfast

it was powered by General Electric CF.6 engines, rarely found on a 747, instead of the more common Pratt & Whitney JT9Ds. Iran Air's engine shop had plenty of experience with GE engines thanks to its large fleet of A300s and A310s so EP-IAI was a good fit and provided a decade of valuable service for Iran's flag carrier.

Other than a handful of short-term leases and four Iran Air Force 747-2J9F freighters that occasionally operated on behalf of the national airline, that was the 747 fleet that Iran Air flew into the 1980s, the 1990s, and indeed into the twenty-first century.

As the years rolled on, Iran's civil air fleet became more and more unusual, as other airlines retired their old jets and replaced them with more modern, digital machines. By the turn of the century, Iran had become a playground for aviation enthusiasts, as it became the only country in the world where it was still possible to fly on a 707, a 727, and a 747 Classic. Even the extra capacity brought in to meet expanding demand on domestic runs was interesting – a diverse fleet of Tupolev Tu-154s from Russian airlines on damp lease (meaning aircraft and pilots provided by lessor; cabin crew provided by the lessee) and even the odd Ilyushin Il-62 and Yakovlev Yak-42.

I made several trips to Iran to experience Persian hospitality at its best, and fly on a classic while I could.

▲ On November 23, 2014, I was onboard a special enthusiasts charter flight organised by Air Events who chartered EP-IAC, Iran Air's last 747SP, which flew clockwise around Tehran for an hour. Here are some scenes of celebration on board!

▲ After landing in Mumbai at the end of my last Iran Air 747SP flight. If it's people that make the difference, this airline is very special airline indeed.

Some European services were operated by the 747s but after 2009, these routes became Airbus-only: A300-600R and A310-300. The final routes served by Iran Air's classic 747s were to Kuala Lumpur, Tokyo via Beijing (even employing six Japanese cabin crew for this route), Istanbul, and Mumbai. Some of my most memorable flights on Iran Air's classic 747 fleet include a Tehran to Dubai flight on a 747-200B and a Tehran to Kuala Lumpur overnight on a 747SP.

All my flights on Iran Air were marked by very kind cabin crew who did everything they could to make me feel at home, including packing up a set of monogrammed cups, saucers and plates for me after I expressed my desire for a souvenir, letting me move around the aircraft to change seats for a better view, even during taxi, and allowing me to visit the cockpit in flight, including sitting in the jumpseat for landing.

A highlight of my travels with Iran Air was the enthusiasts charter on November 23, 2014 organised by Air Events. I flew with nearly 300 enthusiasts on a one hour clockwise sightseeing flight around Tehran aboard EP-IAC under the command of the 747 fleet manager, Captain Moghadam. The atmosphere onboard was magic, with foreign visitors and members of Iran's vibrant spotting community coming together to celebrate a legend. The cockpit door stayed open for the whole flight, with a long line in the upper deck and on the spiral staircase of enthusiasts waiting to catch a glimpse of the crew at work in a classic analogue cockpit. The aisles were so busy in flight that it was impossible for the kind and patient cabin crew to distribute the gift packs until after we landed – a certificate, a portion of local saffron, and a Persian-style tablecloth.

EP-IAC flew on for another eighteen months, and I was able to fly on her one more time to Mumbai, until finally withdrawn from use and parked at Tehran Imam Khomeini in early 2016. Finally, on May 22, 2016, she operated Iran Air's last-ever 747 movement on a short positioning flight across town to Tehran Mehrabad for storage and scrapping with her three SP comrades.

▲ Upper deck is all economy

▲ The 747's original spiral staircase

▲ Those JT9Ds keep on turning

▲ The sweep of analogue dials in the cockpit of a classic 747

▲ Always a kind welcome from Iran Air crews

▲ After a long daylight cruise, landing at dusk at Tehran IKA

Iran Air 747 Fleet List

747SP-86
EP-IAA 12/3/76
EP-IAB 10/5/76
EP-IAC 27/5/77 (last flying)
EP-IAD 12/7/79 (del all white after the revolution)

747-286B
EP-IAG 5/10/76
EP-IAH 14/3/77

747-186B
EP-IAM 20/6/79 (del all white after the revolution)
EP-IAN not built
EP-IAP not built
EP-IAR not built

747-230B
EP-IAI 18/3/08 (originally del LH 25/2/82)

Iran's Independent Airline: Mahan Air

▲ Mahan Air is the only carrier to offer domestic passengers in Iran a business class product, including a lounge

After winning their defensive war against Saddam Hussein's invasion (1980 to 1988), Iran's population and economy boomed, and with it came a huge rise in demand for air travel. The first independent airline to be founded was Mahan Air, named after a historical city in the southern province of Kerman, 1991. The airline started with a patchwork fleet of Tu-154Ms and Il-76s, followed by a trio of Airbus A300s.

In 2008, a pair of ex-Air France 747-300s were purchased, originally delivered to French carrier UTA, to better serve international routes out of Tehran to European cities neglected by Iran Air such as Dusseldorf and Manchester, heavily-trafficked hops to Istanbul and Dubai, the lucrative leisure route to Bangkok, and domestic flying such as Tehran to Mashhad (the Middle East's busiest domestic city pair), to Bandar Abbas on the Persian Gulf, and to the holiday resort island of Kish.

The interiors were smartly turned out in the airline's signature dark green, although decorative maps on the bulkheads illustrating French overseas territories in the Caribbean such as Guadeloupe and Martinique remained unchanged from their UTA days. Although proud that their airline has joined the jumbo club, Mahan only roster 12 cabin crew to work on the 747, making a short flight with over 400 passengers hard work, especially as Iranian domestic airlines serve a hot meal on all sectors and in all classes, despite the short flight time.

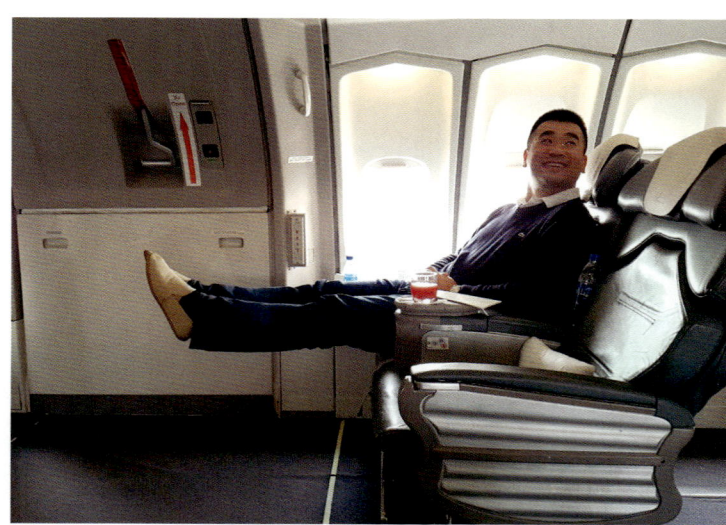

▲ Upper deck on the 747-300 has the spacious business class cabin

▲ Before boarding with Shahram Sharifi, one of Iran's most famous aviation ambassadors

Worth noting also is Mahan's acquisition of three ex-United 747-400s, acquired via an Armenian carrier called Blue Sky Airlines. After a short burst of initial flying in 2008, they were grounded at Tehran's Imam Khomeini airport for a decade with all traces of the Mahan livery and even their registrations removed because of a controversy regarding their ownership. In late 2019 they were finally reactivated.

Mahan Air's 747s are mostly confined to domestic runs, from Tehran Mehrabad to the holy city of Mashhad on the Afghan border (the busiest domestic route in the Middle East) and Bandar Abbas on the Persian Gulf. They are the only airline to offer a domestic business class product in Iran with a lounge and generous catering, for a surcharge of just $50.

Mahan Air is just one more reason to visit beautiful Iran again and again. Merci and mamoon!

▲ All economy on the main deck, from the nose

▲ Generous business class meal for a short flight

Cathay Pacific: Spirit Of Hong Kong

Like some other chapters, the pictures are from Sam's trips, and the text is written by CK based on his own flight experience.

Cathay Pacific occupies a special place in the hearts of Australians, as Hong Kong is a major stopover for Aussies travelling to or from Europe – a place to spend a few days en route to get a suit or some shirts made, shop in the markets, stroll up Nathan Road, flag down a G&T at the Peninsula. Many Cathay pilots are Australian, some gravitating directly from flying school, others as refugees from the shutdown of Ansett Australia in 2001. Along with Singapore Airlines and Thai International, Cathay Pacific could be considered an Australian flag carrier, so important is the market to the airline's bottom line, and so important to the mobilisation of multiple generations of Australians.

When Cathay announced the last flight of the 747 would take place on the Haneda route on October 1, 2016, this Australian couldn't resist one last flight on a Cathay 747, and booked a ride using British Airways points on CX543, on September 27, 2016.

I stayed overnight at the Royal Park Hotel which is located right inside Haneda's modern international terminal, so I needed to take no more than a few steps from the hotel reception area to Cathay's check in desk. Although I was booked in Economy, I was able to use the first class check-in thanks to my Emerald (top tier) status with fellow oneworld alliance member British Airways.

With 55 premium cabin seats on the jumbo, there was a line at the dedicated first and business class check-in counters, but Cathay's capable ground staff dealt with each customer swiftly and I was soon checked in by a friendly and helpful agent despite two legs on different bookings, and my two heavy bags were tagged through to Manchester, clearing the way ▶

▲ Old school herringbone in business class but always a stylish ride in the upper deck of the jumbo

▲ The spacious nose of the jumbo for Cathay Pacific's luxurious first class product

for an uninterrupted nine hour stay in Cathay's lounges at Hong Kong.

Cathay have laminated seat maps of the fleet at the check-in desk to show passengers where they're sitting and what's on offer (why don't every airline do this?). I wanted to steal the 747 seat map but with three days left of 747 operations it might still be missed. I can only assume it's now in the possession of a sticky-fingered enthusiast who was among the last to check-in on October 1. With help from the seat map, I picked a seat down the back in one of the outer pairs, where 3-4-3 becomes 2-4-2.

After clearing security, I used my BA gold status to spend an hour in the Cathay lounge on the top floor, commanding an impressive view of airfield action. The approach to land involves a low-level turn to join finals very late, and every minute another jet, many of them widebody 777s and 787s on domestic runs, curved around to touch down outside the panoramic windows. A choice of Chinese or Japanese breakfast was offered, cooked to order and signalled when ready with a radio-controlled buzzer. I was pleased to see our 747 wasn't the only one of its kind on the move, as a Thai jumbo landed from Bangkok.

I wandered down to gate 145 where a familiar sight awaited. The jade-green jumbo sat nose-in to the loading area, two jetbridges attached, cockpit and upper deck presiding over the surroundings. Passengers took pictures from the glassed-in boarding area — all Hong Kong locals, one of the most mobile populations in the world, have a love affair with the 747, and Japan too, since JAL and All Nippon at their peak operated more than 200 machines including a few dozen dedicated to domestic runs, the biggest national fleet of jumbos in the world.

At this point, the very end of Cathay's 747 operations, the fleet was down to three machines – B-HUI, -HUJ and HKT. The first two were delivered new to Cathay as 747-467s, and the latter an ex-Singapore Airlines -412. From spying the registration painted on the nosegear, today's CX543 was to be operated by B-HKT, distinctive also for the Pratt & Whitneys under the wing, as opposed to Cathay's original Rolls-Royce powered fleet.

Nonetheless, there was no sign of a previous owner. Boarding the aircraft definitely induced a grand and peaceful state, the soft green tones reinforcing the Cathay corporate brand which stands for reliability and luxury. With retirement of the fleet in the works for some time, the 747s never received the most up-to-date hard product installed on their latest Cathay 777-300ERs, sticking with the herringbone business class that has now been replaced everywhere else (except Air Canada, Virgin Atlantic and Air New Zealand). But the kind-hearted welcome and clean aircraft appearance suggested a machine in the prime of its life; most passengers would never have guessed it was three days from retirement.

Demonstrating the appeal of the Tokyo to Hong Kong route, with over 20 flights from Narita and Haneda every day, almost all of the 747's 359 seats were occupied (breaking down as 9 first, 46 business, 26 premium economy, 278 economy) and we were ready to push back for an on-time departure at 1035 local time.

We made a long tour of the airfield, rolling past the Nippon maintenance hangars where the latest 787s received some attention, then out on a pier to the new runway 05 which extends into Tokyo Bay on stilts in the water. With a roar from the four massive PW4000 engines, we were rolling. After a 30 second race down the runway, the nose rose into the air and the whole machine levitated magically upwards. As Japan fell away beneath, we rolled into a series of turns to set course to the west for our four-and-a-half hour trip to Hong Kong.

Soon after the seatbelt signs were switched off, a crew member announced that Mount Fuji was visible off the right side of the aircraft. I hopped out of my seat and found a free window on the other side, and there it was, rising 12,388 feet, the tallest mountain in Japan and in the words of UNESCO, "Inspiring artists and poets and the object of pilgrimage for centuries." I'd seen it covered in snow before, but at the end of a hot summer, it was somehow futuristic and intimidating, this enormous yet mute black pyramid. Photos were

▲ Let's fly to Hong Kong

▲ Miso soup to start

▲ Grilled sea bream appetiser

▲ Grilled Spanish mackerel, saikyou-yaki style

▲ Tempura and seafood plate

▲ Sweet dessert to finish

snapped by passengers and then as Fuji-san slipped out of sight we settled down for an early lunch, served on trays in economy.

I had the Chinese beef option, which came with a prawn cocktail appetiser, a bread roll and a Kit-Kat, washed down with green tea and water. Although fairly basic, it was tasty and filling. Trays were cleared away and I sat back to read and listen to the dull roar of the queen of the skies cutting through the upper atmosphere at over 500mph, 35,000 feet above the East China Sea.

All too soon the distant thunder of the engines died away and a momentary sense of weightlessness signalled the top of descent into Chep Lap Kok airport. As our altitude on the flight map began unwinding, the captain came on the PA and paid tribute to the type's long history in Cathay service and that the crew would be sad to see the end of passenger service for the jumbo – a classy touch.

▲ My co-author who wrote this text flew economy, while I flew in first. Doesn't matter, a Cathay Pacific jumbo in any class is a destination in itself

Soon we were down in the haze of Hong Kong and the skyline came into view as the flaps were extended for landing. With a thump the wheels were lowered and we were on finals for runway 25R. We returned to earth with a rattle and a smudge of blue smoke whipping out from under the wing. Spoilers rose to dump the lift and settle the full weight of the jumbo onto the wheels for effective braking; we smoothly decelerated to walking pace and turned off towards the bustling terminal area for parking, 15 minutes ahead of our scheduled 1500 arrival time.

As passengers deplaned I asked if I could visit the cockpit and was escorted up the stairs to meet the pilots. We had a brief chat about the 747's planned delivery flights to California and Bruntingthorpe UK for scrapping while the cabin crew took turns sitting in the pilots' seats for photos as it was their last work trip on a jumbo.

The captain then invited me to sit in the captain's seat for a photo of my own. I thought of all the men and women who had sat here during the hundred thousand hours B-HKT had clocked up since it was rolled off the line at Seattle in December 1992 for Singapore Airlines, and, since April 2000, Cathay Pacific – landings at dawn and dusk, long nights across the Pacific, daylight crossings of oceans, deserts, whole continents, in or above all imaginable weather conditions.

The last passenger flight, also CX543, operated as promised on October 1 2016, a frenzy of avgeek enthusiasm and nostalgia for the end of an era. The following week, on October 8, Cathay operated a special sightseeing flight for 359 employees, each of whom donated HK$747 to the Hong Kong Breast Cancer Foundation, flight number CX8747, with the airline using social media to advise the public of the best vantage points to watch the aircraft fly over the city it had served for decades.

20 747 freighters (six 747-400ERFs and 14 747-8Fs) fly on at Cathay but the era of 747 passenger flights at Cathay Pacific is over; my last trip on one was a memorable way to say goodbye.

History Special: Cathay Pacific

Cathay Pacific was founded as the Roy Farrell Export-Import Co. in 1946 by a pair of ex-military pilots, Sydney de Kantzow (an Australian) and Roy Farrell (an American) to serve Hong Kong; the name Cathay Pacific was chosen later the same year during a late-night session at the Manila Hotel. (Incidentally, in Chinese, the airline is aptly called "grand and peaceful state".) Because of Hong Kong's status as a British Dependent Territory from the mid-1800s until handed back to China on July 1, 1997, it didn't enjoy statehood and therefore was unable to negotiate much in the way of long haul air treaties, and most of the flying from there was done by British Airways. In Cathay Pacific's early days, it was only able to secure traffic rights to local ports such as Taipei, Bangkok, Singapore, Manila, Jakarta and down to Australia.

The fleet included Douglas DC-3 and Lockheed Electra propliners, followed by early jets such as the Convair CV-880A (a fleet of nine, mostly acquired from VIASA and Japan Airlines) and the Boeing 707 (a fleet of 15, mostly acquired from Northwest Orient Airlines). Cathay Pacific moved up a league in 1975 with the purchase of two L-1011 Tristar widebodies from Lockheed, a love affair which resulted in the procurement of 19 more second hand examples, mostly from Eastern Airlines in the USA but also British Airways, Air Lanka, Court Line and Air Transat. These were L-1011-1s with limited range, and Cathay Pacific was still restricted to the local region.

The big breakthrough came in 1980 when Cathay Pacific finally secured traffic rights to serve London, and received its first Boeing 747-267B on July 20, 1979, Rolls-Royce engines not only pacifying its colonial masters in the United Kingdom but also for compatibility with the Tristar fleet. The registration displayed local pride: VR-HKG. After being inaugurated on the Sydney run in August and bringing extra capacity to local routes within Asia, the jumbo's London Gatwick debut (via Bahrain) took place the following year, on July 16, 1980.

The fleet of 747-200s expanded to 27 aircraft: 15 people movers and 12 dedicated freighters. Cathay Pacific opened transpacific service to Vancouver in 1983 and to San Francisco in 1986. Half a dozen 747-367s joined the fleet starting in 1985, bringing extra capacity in the stretched upper deck, but incorporating the same cockpit, wing and engines as the -200 – a "minimum change" upgrade. A major evolution to the 747 was in the works, driven by customers including Cathay Pacific, and 1989 Boeing unveiled the 747-400 which went on to become the best-selling variant of the jumbo, arriving just in time for the post-Cold War peace dividend of the 1990s. Cathay Pacific bought 18 passenger models and 12 freighters directly from Boeing and, in the 2000s, another seven ex-Singapore Airlines 747-412 Megatops despite having different Pratt & Whitney powerplants.

The 747 in Cathay Pacific's jade green colours was a staple at airports across Asia and further afield as the airline took its place among the biggest travel brands in the world. In 1998, one of the 747-467s operated the inaugural flight into Hong Kong's Chep Lap Kok airport which replaced the famous but undersized Kai Tak, with a 15-hour, 35 minute flight from New York's JFK via the North Pole. By the mid-2000s Cathay Pacific jumbos were operating daily passenger service at cities as distant from Hong Kong as New York, Johannesburg, Frankfurt, Rome and Dubai, as well as multiple frequencies to strongholds such as London, Los Angeles and across Australia. Due to the volumes on local routes in the region, the 747s were mainstays on trips to Bangkok, Singapore, Beijing, cities in Japan, plus of course the "golden route" to Taipei.

The first deliveries of the twin-engined 777-300ER to Cathay Pacific came in late 2007 and the writing was on the wall for the jumbos. By 2014 the passenger fleet of 747-400s was down to half a dozen, and its last long haul destination was its first US destination: San Francisco, which ended on September 1. After that 747s were only used ad hoc to regional cities such as Taipei, Bangkok, Bali and Singapore when traffic demanded the extra capacity, with one just route still scheduled, the evening Hong Kong to Tokyo Haneda CX542, returning to base the following morning as CX543.

Despite being rocked by politics and the current pandemic, today Cathay Pacific remain one of the world's premier travel brands, with their jade green fleet of heavy twins flying to five continents with style and grace.

Air-India 747-400 Maharaja Service

▲ Boarding via stairs at Jeddah. I was stopped and told that no photos were allowed on the ramp.

I didn't want to fly the conventional A320 or B777 from the UAE direct to Mumbai. After some exploration of the best way to fly, I decided to try the soon-to-be-retired Air-India B747-400 from Jeddah via Hyderabad to Mumbai. I circumvented the Saudi visa requirement by connecting airside in Jeddah from Dubai. As a result of my non-conventional routing, my journey from Dubai to Mumbai was over 16 hours with two stops! Jeddah is a massive facility but the channel for transit passengers is almost non-existent and requires finding an official to take your passport to the airline staff for your onward flight, returning after a long wait with your boarding pass. Somehow I managed to get through the layers of officialdom and was airside by 10pm for my 747 flight to India.

Boarding commenced around 11pm. Passengers were brought by bus from the terminal as there are no airbridges at Jeddah. Upon boarding, I had the pleasure of having the whole jumbo nose area and first class cabin to myself. All at once, I felt like a Maharaja onboard!

Five minutes before midnight, we commenced pushback off our remote parking stand and started engines. Only three minutes later we had completed our taxi to the threshold of runway three-four left. "All crew to be seated," came the announcement from the cockpit, with flight attendants rushing to stop what they were doing in the galleys or in the aisles and get strapped into the jumpseats.

Three minutes after midnight, Captains O. Singh and V. Singh pushed the throttles to the max and we skyrocketed out of Jeddah, followed by a large bank over the city and its famous King Fahd Fountain, jetting a plume of illuminated water 300 metres (1,000 feet) into the air above the Red Sea. We rolled out on an easterly heading, towards India.

I was really pleased and impressed with the 747-400's climb performance. The whole cabin was dimmed

▲ First Class cabin of Air-India's 747-400. Only 12 seats in all.

▲ Your choice of curry masala (eggplant), chicken curry, lamb kebab, vegetable biryarni, chicken biryarni and chicken korma with mint yogurt.

▲ Business Class is located on the upper deck. A total of 26 lie-flat seats with nice side wall decorations.

▲ Economy Class. Both sectors were full.

on takeoff and I really enjoyed the climb out and majestic turn performed by the 18 year-old Jumbo Jet. What a feeling at midnight in the clear sky flying out of Jeddah! Long live the Queen of the Skies!

Flight time to Hyderabad was four hours, 35 minutes through the night. We landed in daylight, with a ground transit time in Hyderabad of an hour and a half. I did not have to deplane in Hyderabad. During transit, I was able to roam free around the cabin to take some more pictures.

Some passengers disembarked while domestic passengers joined us, lucky to experience the majesty of the 747 on the short domestic hop to Mumbai, which was only an hour and a quarter. Including the transit in Hyderabad, my time onboard the 747 all the way through from Jeddah to Mumbai was more than eight hours, compared to a mere three hour direct flight from the UAE to Mumbai.

The kind purser ever gave me a whole bottle of champagne to take home with me, due to consumption of alcohol on flights to and from Saudi Arabia being forbidden. I must have looked thirsty from my Jeddah transit!

At three minutes after ten in the morning Mumbai time, VT-ESN slammed hard onto runway one-four, using all its braking power to come to a halt at the very end of the runway. I felt a tremendous welcome to India, and best of all, I arrived in style on-board an Air-India B747-400 with their world-famous Maharaja Service!

▲ Maharajah in the cruise between Hyderabad and Mumbai

Syrian Special Performance

In March 2008, I was visiting the Middle East and jumped at the opportunity to fly on a Syrianair B747SP to Damascus, and experience domestic flights to Aleppo and Latakia aboard the Soviet-built Tupolev Tu-134 and Yakovlev Yak-40. However, things don't always go according to plan...

Syrianair was an unusual 747SP customer because their route network never included any long haul destinations, so the special performance of this unique machine was never put to the test. Although the range was a factor when choosing the type – there was a plan to jointly operate to New York with Royal Jordanian, with Damascus or Amman as the city of origin depending on the day of the week. The main attraction for the 747SP for Syrianair was the reduced capacity, as modern day Syria has never been a mainstream tourist draw, and with a moribund command economy, not much business traffic either. The New York route never materialised, leaving the pair of Syrian 747SPs to operate scheduled to London to the west, Delhi to the east, and subbing for 727s on busy travel days to local destinations in the Gulf.

I was looking forward to flying on this old school airline, but just minutes prior to boarding in Dubai, our Syrianair 747SP 'went tech', short for technical. More accurately, short for a technical problem.

We were told Syrianair needed to fly in their own engineers from Damascus to fix the plane. At 1:30 in the morning, nearly ten hours late, we boarded the plane. However, it wasn't smooth sailing as some passengers were missing and their bags have to be found in the cargo bays in the belly of the jumbos and offloaded.

▲ Angry passengers demanding answers from the captain

▲ Broken duct that delayed our flight travels back to Damascus in the sideways galley

▲ Boarding at last

▲ Views of Syria are on the bulkheads of all Syrianair's vintage Boeings

▲ Old school but cosy business class in the upper deck of the 747SP

Some passengers broke out an argument with flight crew over the treatment of the delay and the captain locked himself in the cockpit, announcing that anyone who doesn't want to co-operate should leave the plane. There were heated arguments in the passenger cabin; the main complaint from passengers was about the misinformation and lack of dignity in the handling of the lengthy delay.

The technical problems were fixed by replacing a damaged pressurisation duct, with the necessary part coming from another 747SP stored in nearby Sharjah. We took off eventually at 3am. The crew saw us as the only foreigners onboard and were kind enough to offer us row 1A and 1B. I was so tired after the 11 hours delay but was awake for the dinner.

Meanwhile, Damascus was gearing up to host the Arab Summit in the next few days, so by the time we were on our way, the airport at our destination was closed to all traffic, so we were diverted to land in Aleppo, actually the largest city in Syria. The bus ride to the capital added an extra seven hours to the journey, which should have been a quick couple of hours' hop, but turned into an epic.

The Syrianair 747SP was a rare bird to fly on, and sometimes things don't go perfectly to plan, but spontaneity and surprises are what life can be all about. Truly an interesting tale to tell!

My Flight On A Private 747SP

▲ In the cockpit before engine start

▲ Hydraulic pressure rising on systems one and four as we bring our jumbo to life

▲ Four good engines and we're ready to taxi

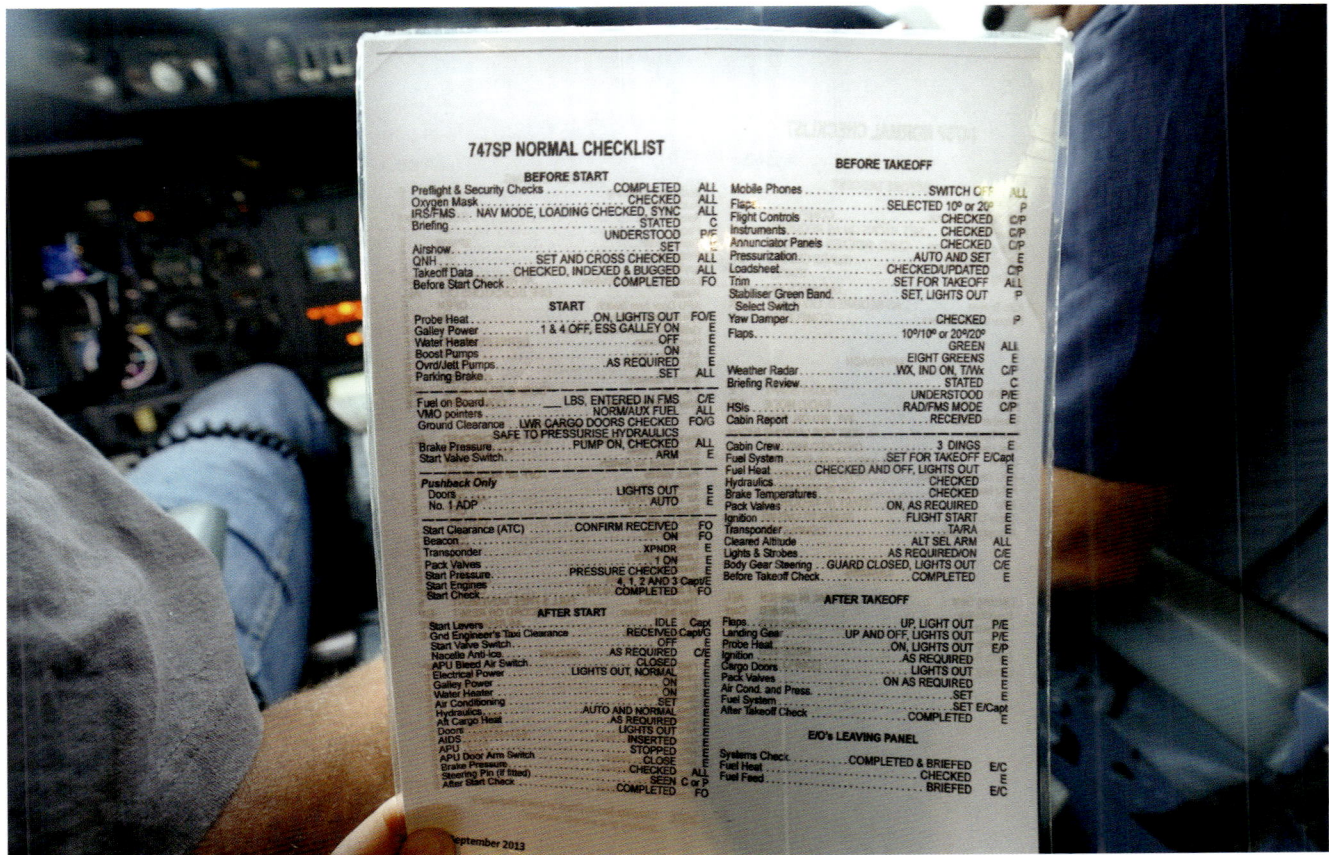

▲ While some tasks are accomplished from memory, a printed checklist is used at every stage of flight in an aircraft as complex as a Boeing airliner

Back in July I received a message from a Twitter account called Airplane Ben. He told me that he owns a Boeing 747SP and that he wanted me to fly on it. Most of you would be thinking that this was a joke, but I did some research and it turned out that there was indeed a Boeing 747SP parked in Hamilton, Ontario, Canada (I love how Canadians love giving their cities nicknames and The Hammer is no exception).

From then on, I followed Ben's tweets with interest. After seeing a tweet about a successful engine run and plans for a heavy C check, I knew that my B747SP dream was getting closer. The plane was ready to leave storage in Hamilton after spending almost a year on the ground.

While I was in Mauritius on a filming project with Air Mauritius, I got my invitation to join the flight of the B747SP. There was not a lot of details or clarity, and definitely no certainty, but I decided to take the chance.

The timing was tight; super tight. I still couldn't believe that I managed to make it all the way from Africa to The Hammer within 24 hours. I flew from Mauritius to Paris and as soon as I landed, I bought my ticket to fly to Toronto on the same day, October 3; Hamilton is an easy 45 minute drive from Toronto.

I met up with the maintenance crew in the hotel and was told that everything was ready, just waiting on one document from the Federal Aviation Authority aka the FAA, the regularity and advocacy body for anything and everything that takes to the air over the United States. I learned that during storage, some equipment had been removed, such as radios, to keep them safe from the harsh elements of Canadian weather; and to reactivate the aircraft, technicians had overseen engine runs, checking altimeters, sensors, and all the aircraft systems.

▲ Welcome aboard, my private 747!

It can be uncertain with aviation until the last minute. The bigger the risk you take, the bigger the reward when it works. But there is always room for disappointment if it doesn't happen.

I was preparing myself for the eventuality that the flight wouldn't take place the following day, which would mean I would have to reschedule my busy work diary.

While we were still waiting for the so-called 'fly-wire' document from the FAA, the pilots and flight engineer arrived at Hamilton airport. We were taken out to the plane to start preparations for our flight, all the time hoping to receive the fly-wire document we needed.

This B747SP-21 was built in 1979 and delivered to Pan Am as N539PA. In 1986, it was transferred to United Airlines as N148UA when United made a billion-dollar buy-out of all Pan Am's Pacific route authorities and the widebody jets needed to fly them. A decade later, in 1995, it was acquired by Qatar Amiri Flight and converted to a private head of state jet transport, where it served as VR-BAT and latterly VP-BAT, finally replaced by a state-of-the-art Boeing 747-8i BBJ in 2018.

While the crew were busy with documentation and planning, these were tense moments for me, not knowing whether we would be cleared for takeoff or not.

To fill in the time, I was given a tour of the cockpit and the main equipment centre located underneath the main floor and accessed by a narrow staircase. Radios, avionics and navigation instruments are all stored here.

Around midday, the good news finally arrived! We had received the 'fly-wire' and the aircraft was cleared to fly to the Pinal Air Park in Pinal, Arizona. Everyone was relieved, and started the final preparations for departure.

At 13:15, the ground engineer team bid farewell to the plane and the door was closed. I was the only passenger.

▲ Main meeting room

I was sitting behind the pilots on the jumpseat. It was amazing to watch the pilots and flight engineer working with this analogue hardware, manually starting one engine after another. The four Pratt & Whitney engines came to life with an amazing sound!

At 13:42 the B747SP was airborne, after nearly a year in storage! The spooling sound of four JT9D-7A engines was music to my ears.

Flight time from Hamilton to Marana was scheduled to be exactly four hours. Once the plane reached its cruising level of 38,000 ft and cruising speed of Mach .86, I went downstairs to walk around and took a lot of photos/videos. Let's have a tour of the interior!

The upper deck has 12 'La-Z-Boy' deep recliner seats and a small galley behind. Due to the curvature of the fuselage crown, there are no overhead bins in the ceiling; instead. Instead, there are side bins next to the windows on each side.

▲ Unlike the main deck, the upper deck looks a lot like the business class of a normal airliner

▲ Sleeping in such luxury would be a waste!

I walked downstairs via the iconic spiral staircase unique to the 747 Classic to have a look at the lower deck. The master bedroom and bathroom are located in the nose area of the B747SP. There is also a private working desk and sofa in the master bedroom. The bed can go up and down with a remote control.

Given that this aircraft is from a former Qatar Amiri Flight aircraft, there is the Majlis near the entrance of door 2. Majlis means Council in Arabic and refers to special gatherings for administrative, social or religious matters in the Islamic world. You can probably guess who normally sits in the blue colour 'throne' seat,

▲ The bathroom is bigger than some apartments

▲ Majlis, or meeting room, for business of state

which can recline to 180 degrees flat with a push of an electronic button. But on this flight, it was my seat!

Continuing the tour by walking down the long side aisle, the next room is the dining/conference room. The B747SP fuselage is so wide, it truly feels like I am inside a flying palace.

Right behind the dining room, there is another small private office with a private toilet and shower.

The remaining section was filled with seats for the entourage, security, and servants. Given that the plane is 40 years old, the interiors have been well maintained. All the controls I tried worked flawlessly.

It was a really strange flight. I was the only person on the entire lower deck. No other passengers or crew were present. I used the four hour flight time to try out literally every single seat in all the areas.

The cloud bank below us gradually gave way to a clear sky as we continued to head southwest. During the descent into Marana we encountered some wild wind, which is quite common in the open desert area. The TCAS system was active and warned 'traffic, traffic' nearby as we made our approach.

We landed at Marana around 14:45 local time with a flight time of four hours and a minute. Sunny weather, with a temperature of nearly 100 degrees Fahrenheit (37 Celcius) welcomed us. The B747SP was scheduled for a C-Check in Marana and was waiting for a new buyer.

▲ Classic JT9Ds in flight

I love the 747, I love luxury travel and I love classic aviation, so what could be better than flying on a vintage 747SP private jet with a full head of state configuration? Even better, I had the whole plane to myself!

One additional aspect of the flight I relished was the unusual city pair. This was almost certainly the only time Hamilton and Marana have ever been linked by air nonstop.

I had been following the reactivation of this Boeing 747SP for some time. There were always going to be risks that the flight may not have happened, due to one problem or another, but I am so glad that my gamble had completely paid off! I think this flight has raised my aviation adventures to a new level. It is simply my best flight experience in 2019.

▲ More meeting space

Corsair Et Le Jumbo

France, until the middle of the 20th century, ruled over an empire that included large areas of Africa (including Algeria, Tunisia, Côte d'Ivoire, Mali, Mauritania, Niger, Senegal, Chad), the Middle East (including Syria and Lebanon), the Americas (Québec, Louisiana, Haiti, parts of Brazil), and Indian Ocean islands such as Madagascar and the Seychelles. All of these today are independent nations. The fragments that have remained are not just dependent territories, like, say, members of the British Commonwealth, for whom Queen Elizabeth II is head of state but are sovereign states. They are actually France. Their citizens are French citizens, European Union citizens, they vote in French elections, and enjoy the exact same rights as a Parisian, despite being thousands of miles away. The territories are grouped under the appellation France d'outre-Mer, or Overseas France.

The most populated and well known are Guadeloupe, French Guiana (main city Cayenne) and Martinique in the Caribbean, and Réunion in the Indian Ocean. Consequently, there is a large air travel market between these island satellites and the mother ship of metropolitan France, consisting of both VFR (visiting friends and relatives) traffic and tourism, as the islands are blessed with beautiful beaches, warm weather, and French culture. One of the many fascinating aspects of these flights is that, despite being up to ten hours

(photo by Guy Van Herbruggen)

long and covering thousands of miles of ocean, they are domestic flights, so France and indeed all EU citizens can board with just a driver's licence or national ID card, and they operate from Paris's domestic airport, Orly, as opposed to the international hub, Charles De Gualle.

Air France have served these destinations since the dawn of long haul flight, with propliners, 707s, 747s, and today a dedicated subfleet of high-density Boeing 777-300ERs with room for 468 passengers. The opening up of the French air travel sector to independent airlines made room for competitors, initially AOM French Airlines (Air Outre-Mer) who operated up to 15 McDonnell Douglas DC-10s on their long haul routes, but with the airline's bankruptcy in 2001, the market was wide open again.

Corse Air was founded in 1981 by the prominent Rossi family on the Mediterranean island of Corsica and began flying to the mainland with a small fleet of second hand French-built Caravelle jets. In 1990 the airline was bought by French tour operator Nouvelles Frontières and began expanding into a holiday and charter airline with worldwide traffic rights and a pair of ex-Pan Am 747-100s (one of which went on to star in the movie Executive Decision).

This flirtation with the 747 turned into a hot-blooded French love affair, with two more 747-100s ▶

▲ Boarding complete and ready to set sail for the Caribbean. The main deck is configured for economy class, including the nose, usually reserved for first class

▲ Even though Corsair is a low cost leisure carrier, they are also French, and that means a good quality and generous main meal

▲ Small business class cabin in the forward half of the upper deck, with 12 flat beds

joining from Air France, followed by a pair of ex-KLM 747-200Bs and one from Iberia, and even an oddball ex-South African Airways 747SP whose range was useful to inaugurate nonstop flights to Réunion, a 5,802 mile / 9,338 kilometre trip from Orly.

Singapore Airlines are famous for selling their planes after only a few years of service to keep their fleet young, so at the end of the 1990s Corsair jumped in and bought five -300s from Singapore, still in the prime of their lives, replacing the mix-and-match -100, -200B and SP fleet and adding seats with the stretched upper deck adding capacity of the -300 Big Top. This was fortuitous timing, as Nouvelles Frontières was purchased in 2000 by German tourism giant TUI, expanding to new leisure destinations such as Bangkok, Cancún, Montréal, Havana, Los Angeles, San Francisco, and even as far as Nouméa (New Caledonia) and Papeete (Polynesia) via California, deep in the South Pacific.

Another bargain loomed in 2005 with United replacing part of its 747-400 fleet with 777-200ER twinjets, and Corsair made their move, selling their -300s to Air Atlanta Icelandic and joining the digital revolution with United's mainliners which could effortlessly reach the furthest points in the French solar system.

The ex-United 747-400s had seating for 587 seats, the highest seat count on any 747, even higher than the 747-400Ds used on Japanese domestic flights. The addition of two pilots, 22 cabin crew, off duty employees hitching a ride in empty jump seats pushed the total past 600, but because these birds were mostly flying families on holiday, it was normal to carry as many as 30 babies in mums' laps, for a total of 640 souls on board. Mon dieu!

Later in their Corsair careers, the upper deck was converted to a two class premium cabin, with three rows of flat beds for a tiny business class section, and four rows of generous recliners for a tiny premium economy section; plus a slight reshuffle on the main deck, bringing the total number of seats down to 533, but with a full load including babies (the collective noun

▲ Long hours pass gently, cruising across the Atlantic to a tropical paradise

▲ Author Charles Kennedy visiting friendly crew in the small galley at the rear of the upper deck

▲ Second service is just two pieces of chocolate ...and a cup of hot chocolate!

▲ Even though this is an old jet, with a long career at United Airlines before Corsair, it is in immaculate condition, both in the cabin and the cockpit

for which, by the way, is an infantry), that's still nearly 590 souls on board.

The Corsair jumbos were famous for their registrations including F-GSUN, 'SEA and 'SEX. Their final livery, with large titles and a blue rear fuselage and tail emblazoned with the white sails of a yacht, was a great representation of their breezy and friendly culture, and the destinations they flew to – ocean light, sun on saltwater, palm-fringed beach club. In the years when 747s began to disappear from the fleets of the world airlines, a cluster of these ships at the gate at Orly's historic 1961-built Terminal Sud were a notable hold-out, boarding happy families heading to the beach or a (pardon the pun) reunion.

Corsair announced they would not reinstate the 747 fleet after the Covid 19 grounding, and on June 15 2020, the last of the fleet, F-GTUI, landed at Kemble-Cotswold near Bristol in southwest England for scrapping. These birds were planned for retirement in 2021 anyway, over 100,000 hours in their logbooks, to be replaced by A330s. But after such sterling service for United and Corsair, they deserved a more dignified farewell. Alas, such a grand au revoir was not to be, but they will live on in the hearts of the French people, both in Metropolitan France and her far-flung islands.

▲ The silhouette of a 747 is unmistakable

▲ Taxiing at Orly

(Olivier Cabaret)

Flying On A KLM 747-400 Combi

▲ World Business Class in the nose of the 747. The most exclusive cabin in the sky!

▲ Unusual half-width Economy Comfort cabin...

▲ ...because of the lengthways galley

Until its retirement in March 2020, the Boeing 747 was the biggest aircraft in KLM's fleet, since the airline introduced it on the trunk route from Amsterdam to New York back in 1971. Over the years, KLM has operated some unusual 747 variants, including the 747-200SUD (a 747-200B with the stretched upper deck of the -300 as an aftermarket modification), and Combi (a mix of passengers and cargo on the main deck) -300s and -400s, plus -300 and -400 pure freighters.

I took a memorable flight on of KLM's Combis, from Amsterdam to Mexico City, in January 2020. The aircraft PH-BFW City of Shanghai, delivered to KLM in October 2000, making it 19 and a half years old. As well as the cavernous underfloor cargo bays common to all widebody airliners, combis have a partitioned main

▲ Climbing through the clouds, landing lights on

▲ Amenity kit for passengers in World Business Class includes lipbalm, eye mask, socks, toothbrush, moisturiser, earplugs, and a small pen

▲ It's the human factor that turns a good flight into a great one

deck, with passengers in the forward half, and cargo in the rear half of the main deck, with a large side door on the left side of the cabin behind the wing. Sometimes the extra cargo capacity is needed to meet pure volume, but at other times, its high headroom and inflight access makes combis perfect for outsize loads (such as oil drilling equipment or staging for pop concerts), or in the case of my flight to Mexico, large animals such as like elephants or horses.

In KLM service, the 747-400 Combi had passenger accomodation for 35 World Business class, 36 in economy plus (a standard economy product with some extra legroom) and 197 standard economy class sears, for a total of 268 passengers. Behind the partition were seven cargo positions in the rear.

On a wintery day with low cloud and rain, we took off from runway 24 around 3pm, flying low over the Netherlands before turning onto our Great Circle track across the UK with a flight plan that would carry us out over the Atlantic passing Iceland and Greenland, making landfall over Canada, diagonally overflying a big chunk of the USA, and on into Mexico. With our route and winds aloft, the flight time was planned at 11 hours 33 minutes.

The nose and upper deck on the 747 is World Business Class. Nice to be able to fly in luxury in the nose of a jumbo but only pay business class, not first! KLM have an unusual forward galley, which runs along the right side of the plane between doors one and two. This also creates an unusual first economy cabin, with seats and an aisle on the left side of the plane, but midway across the fuselage is a vertical wall. It might sound claustrophobic but it's actually quite cosy!

A full meal was served as we coasted out into our Atlantic crossing. My main course was called Captain's Choice, which turned out to be Dutch pasta filled with Grouper fish.

After the completion of service, I went to the galley to introduce myself to the lovely KLM crew. I explained to them about my passion for aviation and that I had made this special trip just to fly on a KLM 747. They were very happy to show me their workspace and traded a lot of flying stories with me.

▲ Loading into the main deck cargo bay on this rare combi

▲ Conventional payload...

▲ ...and unconventional

With the captain's permission, I was showed the main deck cargo area behind the passenger cabin; accessible by a locked door during the flight. There are a total of seven pallet positions on the main deck. It was my first time inside the B747-400 Combi cargo deck. This was truly a unique experience for me!

We had some special guests in the cargo hold; 13 horses in four separate special containers. There was also a horse groom looking after them. There was plenty of hay inside the containers. The horse groom checked all the horses every two hours and to feed them water. The horses were all very calm; they're frequent travellers! The cargo area was pressurised and fully climate controlled so they had a pretty nice ride.

▲ Soup starter

My backstage tour continued with a visit to the crew rest area, which is located in the rear just after the passenger cabin.

It was almost an entirely daylight flight for the first nine hours or so, as we flew westwards chasing the sun. Finally the sun began setting over Texas near the Gulf of Mexico, as we entered the last phase of the long flight. A second meal was served, it was a rather simple KLM branded cheeseburger!

Before we landed, I took the opportunity to thank the entire crew on my flight. The wonderful KLM crew made me feel extra special and I'm glad I had a chance to fly with them on the 747. 💬

▲ Captains's Choice main course

▲ Second service was a burger, simple and tasty!

▲ Dessert and tea

▲ Sun finally started to set over Texas

ANA's Peoplemover: The 747-400D

Only one country had a large enough domestic air travel market for Boeing to create a customised 747 optimised for hour-long hops with 500 passengers aboard.

Japan is a mountainous island nation of 125 million people, mostly centred on the five 'main islands' of Honshu (which includes Tokyo, Osaka, Nagoya), Hokkaido (famous for beer capital Sapporo), Kyushu (home to Fukuoka and Nagasaki), Shikoku, and Okinawa. (There are a total of 453 inhabited islands in the country.) While Japan's trains are the envy of the world, rail alone cannot meet all of the demand for travel within the country, especially between cities separated by large stretches of water.

Flag carrier Japan Airlines, a keen 747 user across its global route network, collaborated with Boeing from the beginning to create a special variant, with extra structural strength for multiple short flights per day, and less fuel capacity to reduce weight.

Boeing called it the 747 Super Shuttle, which was later abbreviated to 747SR, for Short Range. For use on its domestic network, Japan Airlines received seven 747SR-46s with deliveries beginning in 1973 (one of which later went to NASA and was converted into a 747SCA, to carry Space Shuttles on its back from their desert landing site at Edwards Air Force Base in California to Cape Canaveral in Florida for the next launch).

Meanwhile, Japan's biggest privately-owned airline started out as Nippon Helicopter and Aeroplane Transports Company in 1953. Although it changed its name to All Nippon Airways (ANA), it retained Leonardo da Vinci's famous helicopter design as its logo up until the mid-1980s, and NH its two-letter airline code right up to the present day.

Even in the years that ANA was restricted to only flying within Japan, demand on its all-domestic route network was so great that the airline joined the widebody club in 1974 with the Lockheed L-1011 Tristar, and in 1978 started receiving 747SRs of its own, in fact eclipsing Japan Airlines by eventually operating a large fleet of 17, designated 747SR-81, remaining in service until 2005. Two that left the fleet in 1995 went to start-up Qatar Airways and spent the next four years flying from Doha to Colombo, Male in the Maldives, and London Gatwick via Cairo.

When Boeing launched the digital next-gen 747-400, a short range variant was created for Japan, designated the 747-400D for Domestic. ANA bought 13, and JAL 8. The 747-400D had one clearly visible difference to a regular -400: the lack of upturned winglet. Winglets only increase fuel efficiency in long range cruise; on short hops, they are just extra weight (66 kg / 146 lbs each). ▶

Unlike the 747SR, the 747-400D could be converted to regular 747-400, with reversable winglet attachment points and other elements of flexible hardware. Two JAL 747-446D were converted to regular -446 (JA8955 and JA8957), and in the late 1990s ANA converted two of their 747-481D to regular -481 standard in the late 1990s when they needed more international lift (JA401A and JA402A), then back to -481D in 2002.

In early 2013 I was in Tokyo on business at the same time Sam was in Sapporo on a photo mission, capturing the additional traffic of the winter season, widebodies bringing skiers in from all around Asia. Flying up to CTS, New Chitose / Sapporo, would also give me a chance to fly on a rare 747-400D of ANA (JAL retired all their 747s in 2011).

I awoke at the Excel Tokyu Haneda hotel, whose breakfast room faces the tarmac and has a collection of travel agent sized models, and whose reception exits into the departures concourse at Haneda terminal 2, main tenant ANA. I collected a boarding pass, which in Japan are square and look more like a bus ticket, and went through security without a hitch. Japan excels at every aspect of air travel and effortless ground experience is part of the charm.

I was thrilled to get to the gate and find Pikachu Dreaming, a pop culture icon, ready to fly me up to the ancient island of Hokkaido. Boarding was super efficient and took about six minutes for a half full load. On any other ship, 200-odd passengers would feel like a full house but a 568 seater swallows them whole.

The interior was fully decked out in Pokémon livery, with patterned curtains and headrest covers. It was an early morning flight and I was obviously not on top of my game, as I should have stolen a few headrest covers for the collection, but I did not have my wits about me sufficiently to think of it.

Service was an offering of water or Japanese tea. Although I find green tea in Japan to be quite bitter, and at opposite end of the kind of spectrum where I would normally reside (fizzy water, cream soda, champagne, tequila), the unfamiliar taste is a handy reminder of being in foreign lands, so it was tea for me.

All too soon we were descending over water and snowy landscapes into CTS, where I knew Sam was photographing, and hoped he was out in time to catch Pikachu Dreaming's dramatic arrival. I was sure our masterpiece of a paint scheme would be eye-popping against the white backdrop.

Sam and local spotter Yukihiro Kaneko met me at domestic arrivals right on time, and we were soon in the hire car and racing along a remote perimeter road, through a gate (legally!) and then on foot to the airfield fence on a long snowy access path through bare trees. The spotting location was right under and slightly offset from the final approach path into 01L, zero-one left.

As the day progressed we saw arrivals from Trans Asia Airways (A330), Cathay Pacific (747-400), Eva Air (A330 including Hello Kitty) operated extra or upgauged flights for skiers, as well as the regular domestic widebodies of JAL (777, 767), ANA (747, 777, 767). Air Do is the hometown carrier (the 'Do in the name being the last syllable of Hokkaido) and operate a mix of 737 and 767 which make occasional use of a friendly bear mascot.

The undoubted highlight of the day was the Japan Air Self-Defense Force (JASDAF) Boeing 747. Japan's two head of state jumbos are based at CTS due to its low profile location and uncongested airspace compared to the obvious candidate of Tokyo Haneda. The entire apparatus of state flies on the wings of its head of state transport service, which even when not engaged in formal work must be on high alert at all times for any kind of emergency mission, on which perhaps even the fate of the world may depend. In any airborne scenarios, the pilots must be at the peak of proficiency, so, perhaps counter to expectation, far from sitting in a warm hangar being gently polished by a team of fluffers, these two birds fly almost every day on a training mission of some kind or another.

Sam and I were treated to a series of touch-and-goes by one of the Japanese Air Force Ones which flew with a JASDAF F-15J fighter jet on each wingtip (showing Japan's aeronautical prowess, the J suffix says that they are built under licence by Mitsubishi in Nagoya). After the show seemed to be over, we saw the 747 transiting overhead around 15,000 feet, before eventually returning for a full-stop landing at the conclusion of a three hour sortie.

Sam raced to get back to the terminal for his mid-afternoon Cathay Pacific 747 to Hong Kong. After we parted, I had ample time to check-in for my ANA 747-400D back to Tokyo. On an upper floor of the terminal I found a shop, common to many Japanese airports, selling airline-related memorabilia. This one had lots of items carrying the colourful branding of 1970s US trunk carrier Braniff International who went bust in 1982 but seem to be enjoying a revival in Japan, as there is stationery, stamps, and even luggage, all showing an admirable attention to detail.

By the time we were ready to leave, it was raining, with water running down the windows and refracting the yellow and white electric light coming in from the ramp. For this leg I sat in the upper deck. Usually there is a galley at the rear of the upper deck for serving hot meals to a business class cabin on a long haul flight, but because of the short haul nature of the 747-400D, not having a full upper deck galley allowed an extra row of seats against the back wall of the upper deck, aft of the stairs. So I sat with the stairs leading downwards right in front of me. It seemed like a very interesting place to sit when I saw it on the seatmap and indeed it did not disappoint. The cabin crew offered to move me to one of the many empty rows, suggesting that my perch at the top of the stairs was unpopular and only allocated on the fullest of flights, but I preferred to stay where I was!

A powerful night takeoff was followed by a short southbound cruise back to the capital, where we landed after a steep and dramatic turn in one of Haneda's many unusual arrival paths, curving to avoid built-up areas and industrial infrastructure alike. I walked through Haneda's busy terminal 2, inspired and thrilled by the day in the snowy beauty of Sapporo. As the ANA slogan promises, Inspiration of Japan.

▲ One of All Nippon's beautiful logojets climbing out of Sapporo

The Emir Of Kuwait's Jumbo

▲ Very happy to see this rare 747 at the gate

Kuwait Airways (KU/KAC) operated a sole 747-400 on ad-hoc basis, actually part of Emir of Kuwait's head of state fleet. The 747-400 schedule was never published in advance and always flew as a last-minute aircraft change. Simply put, it was one of the most difficult planes to fly on because of its unpredictability. On random basis, it could operate from Kuwait to Dubai, Jeddah, Cairo, Bombay, Kuala Lumpur, Jakarta, Frankfurt, Geneva or London. It also flew on government missions, as far afield as Ulan Bator, Mongolia on behalf of Kuwait government. The airline can only operate this ship when the government don't require it.

Because of its hybrid mission, it had an unusual layout, with a flying hospital onboard including a full operating theatre, located in the middle of the main deck with seats around it on the two aisles.

During the month of August 2014, I found out Kuwait Airways was using this 747-400 flying between Kuwait and London every two days. The schedule showed AB6 (A300-600R), however if one opened the seat map, it showed a 747! Later on, Kuwait Airways changed the AB6 code to 747 on all GDS. This was the first time since I'd been monitoring and chasing this 747 that the type showed up in GDS and its website. I made a booking straight away, knowing this would be one of the rarest 747-400 to fly with.

The flight to London departs at 12:30pm. With the boarding pass on hand, I proceeded to the Dasman Lounge which welcomes premium passengers flying on the majority of airlines in Kuwait. Interesting that Kuwait Airways did not have its own lounge at its home base. It was spacious with many plush leather sofas. I had

▲ First class cabin in the nose

a quick shower and rest, skipping the excellent food selection. Plenty of hot and cold choices and even various flavour of ice cream was on offer.

I left the lounge a little earlier to the gate. Boarding started at 12:00pm. It was very assuring and satisfying to see a larger than usual tail when walking towards the gate. Yes! It is the 747!

The 747-400 looked awesome from outside, the smart classic Kuwait Airways blue cheat line looking good in the desert sun. Many other passengers also noticed and commented on this unusual aircraft type to London. Showing the diverse missions that a 747 can accomplish simultaneously, there was a white Ferrari sports car being loaded inside the forward cargo hold, and a sick patient on a stretcher was carried onboard.

This is the most exciting moment, to see the interior of this mysterious Kuwati 747 for myself! It was configured with 32 first class seats across Zone A and B with no division, followed by 26 business class seats on both sides with a huge galley in the middle. The rest is economy class on both sides of main deck with the walled-off flying hospital in the middle. The upper deck was strictly off-limits.

I was politely told by the crew that photography is forbidden onboard this aircraft since it belongs to the government of Kuwait. Nevertheless they allowed me taking some food and product pictures.

This plane hadn't seen any changes since in rolled out of factory in the mid 1990s, making it a bit of a time machine, reminding me how first class travel used to be.

▲ Generous buffet-style lunch served seat-side

We took off at 12:50pm from KWI's runway 33L of KWI. Our flight time to London was estimated to be five hours and 50 minutes, initially heading north over Iraq, then onward northwest towards Turkey.

The crew were quite senior (purser appeared to be the youngest, an interesting reversal of roles), mostly from Arabic speaking countries such as Lebanon, Egypt, Morocco with one Kuwaiti lady as well. They were not super friendly so I didn't bother to ask for a crew photo since I could already read from their body language, which was a 'no'.

While the seat and cabin were very old fashioned, the food service was good. Caviar, lamb shawarma, salmon and turkey tartare as starter. (The caviar portion was too small. Later on, during my cabin tour, I saw the crew were eating left over portions, in large scoops!) The main course buffet consisted of pepper steak, grill chicken, Nasi Goreng and grill seafood with rice, vegetable and potato gratin. I loved the old school trolley buffet presentation as you can mix and match, trying a bit of everything.

I would never give up an opportunity to see the rest of the cabin on this rare 747-400. I slept three hours until the second meal was served. It was more like afternoon tea with snacks, sandwiches, shawarmas and cakes. There was plenty of food. Shortly after we started our descent into Heathrow, over the cloudy sky of London. We got special permission to land on runway 27L despite all other traffic land on 27R, which resulted a much shorter taxi to our gate at Terminal 4.

▲ Setting off on a tour of the plane

I was very glad to fly on Kuwait Airways's sole 747-400. I never thought it would be possible in the past. The seating configuration took me back 20 years. First class was fine, the food was great, but can't say the same about the crew. Although I didn't encounter bad service or incident, but I could tell from the body language and the attitude, the crew didn't really want to be there, and treated themselves better than the passengers. This wasn't the case on my other Kuwait Airways flights, which the crew were usually nice and polite. Best thing flying Kuwait Airways is the food served in premium cabins and their old school charm. They are one of the oldest airline brands in the Middle East and have served their tiny city-state nation for decades, so what they lack in modern amenities they make up for with history and reliability.

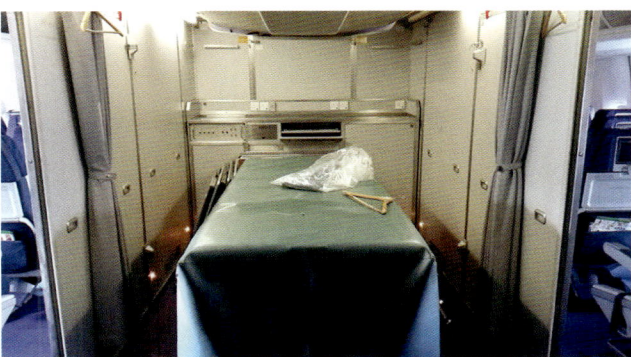

▲ An unusual onboard hospital operating theatre is located in the middle section of economy class

▲ The upper deck is the Emir's private bedroom and office, off limits during commercial operations
(Hospital and upper deck photos by Vin Man)

▲ Economy seating squeezed in around the walled-off hospital, a very unusual arrangement

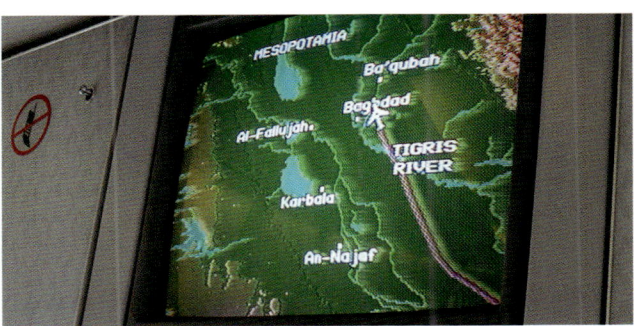

▲ Original moving map shows us passing Baghdad

▲ Very old school first class La-Z-Boy recliners

Air China Domestic 747-8i

The Boeing 747-8i is the latest and last passenger variant of the 747. With airlines moving towards big twins for their long haul hardware, the -8i came late in the 747's life cycle, with only three delivery customers: Lufthansa, Korean Air and Air China, plus a handful of BBJ head of state transports (with three more, not taken up by Rossiya Airlines, to be used as Air Force One, replacing a pair of 747-200Bs delivered in 1990).

I was keen to experience the Air China 747-8i in business class, which is possible for a fraction of the price of an intercontinental trip on one of up to three rotations a day between Beijing Capital airport and Shanghai's old downtown Hongqiao airport, which used to be Shanghai's main gateway but is today only used for domestic flights and to nearby Tokyo (Haneda), Seoul (Gimpo), Taiwan (Songshan), Hong Kong and Macau. Despite being overtaken by the distant and enormous Pudong airport, Hongqiao is still China's seventh busiest airport, and number 45 in the world.

I checked in at the row of dedicated Air China first and business class counters in Beijing Capital's terminal three. By flying business I was able to access the business class lounge in the domestic wing, which serves a few Chinese packaged snacks, instant cup noodles, packaged drinks. There isn't much alcohol on offer.

I took my business class flat bed seat aboard B-2480 in the first row of the nose, row 11. The cabin, the most exclusive address in the sky, felt spacious and ultra modern thanks to the combination of natural daylight and rainbow mood lighting which was on during boarding and taxi. The plane, delivered from Boeing on June 6, 2015, still had a new car feeling.

After a powerful takeoff, a drinks service was immediately followed by a snack service consisting of a fruit plate, dim sum and apricot cake. On some flights there is a full lunch and dinner service with the right timing. ▶

After the meal I went on a quick tour of the rest of the big jet, the biggest ever built by Boeing. Air China's 747-8i (and -400) have a unique layout, which puts the first class cabin in between doors one and two, with business class in the nose and upstairs. It is the only layout where first class is behind business class. The reason for it is that Air China's enormous first class seat is too big to fit in the nose section of the jumbo. Interestingly, to maintain the sense of prestige that comes with flying first, the three rows are numbered 1, 2 and 3, even though business class is physically further forward (and numbered 11 to 15). The upper deck accommodates 30 business class, reached by a stairway with architecture unique to the 747-8i.

All too soon, the rainbow lighting come back on, signaling that it was time to take our seats for approach and landing into Shanghai. A smooth touchdown brought us to the end of our one hour and 40 minute domestic hop. It is awesome to have the honour of flying on a 747-8i on a domestic flight. And the soft product was really good. Air China are a solid world class carrier.

▲ Generous lunch service on a short domestic hop with dumplings, fruit and dessert

▲ Business class in the nose of the jumbo

▲ First class seats are too big to fit in the nose, so they are located on the main deck behind business class

▲ A new staircase design for the 747-8i

▲ Small serving area in the nose

▲ Mood lighting as we approach to land

Qatar Airways 747-8F Freight Giant

In September 2019, I flew on a B747-8 freighter belonging to Qatar Airways, from Hong Kong to their home base, Doha. I learned a lot about cargo operations during this trip. ▶

My trip started in Hong Kong Cargo Super Terminal One which is part of the massive HACTL (Hong Kong Air Cargo Terminals Limited) complex, where logistics are handled for many of the world's biggest names in air freight, including Qatar Airways Cargo. Because Hong Kong Airport is the busiest cargo airport in the world, countless B747 cargo planes operate in and out. With no night curfew, the action never stops.

Goods for onward shipment arrive by road, rail or sea; the cargo will be loaded up on pallets, loaded into bespoke containers, or otherwise prepared for loading into the very precise, contoured dimensions dictated by the interior of the aircraft in which they will travel.

All dedicated widebody freighters have a side loading cargo door, but the Boeing 747 freighter is unique; because the cockpit is perched on the upper deck in the 'bubble', the entire nose opens, creating longitudinal access to the main deck, especially useful for oversize loads such as drilling equipment, pipes, railway locomotives... anything too long to go through the side cargo door and make it round the corner. The Boeing 747-8F has 34 cargo positions for pallets on its main deck, and is able to uplift a total of 135 tons of payload. Each pallet can be as heavy as seven tonnes (and in exceptional circumstances, up to 20 tonnes!). To optimise the space inside the plane, the top of some of the pallets were only a few centimetres clear of the ceiling.

Out of Hong Kong, cargo flights are generally full and are often carrying all sorts of exports from China. Among many other items, my flight was carrying a Rolls Royce Trent 700 engine to be flown on to Madrid to be fitted to an Airbus A330. The engine was given special care as it was loaded aboard through the side door and turned 90 degrees into position on the main cargo deck. The engine was tied down carefully, like all cargo, to avoid any movement during the flight. Interestingly, I learned that one factor an aeroengine manufacturer must consider when they are creating a new powerplant is that it has to fit through the cargo doors of existing freighters so it can be moved around a customer airline's network.

There was a typhoon near Hong Kong on the day of our departure, hampering loading due to occasional downpours of torrential rain and lightning warnings. Rain

▲ On the ground in Hong Kong

▲ Loading the cargo

▲ Cargo included a Rolls-Royce engine for an A330. I had to carry an oxygen bottle at all times on the main deck in case of a loss of cabin pressure.

▲ Full load on the main deck

▲ General Electric GENx engines ready for flight

▲ Cleared for takeoff!

water on some of the pallets needed to be removed before entering the aircraft. It took just over two hours to load up our Boeing 747 to capacity.

I got soaked on the ramp filming for my vlog, but it served to remind me that the show must go on, rain or shine, and the front line ramp workers have to get the plane loaded whatever the weather.

There are narrow stairs from main deck to the upper deck. The cockpit is crewed by two pilots, and has two observer seats for relief pilots or check airmen. Behind that is a small galley, a single lavatory, six passenger seats for positioning crew, a loadmaster, airline executives on an unusual commute, a veteranarian in the event of flying livestock, and rearmost are two bunk beds for crew rest.

Before the flight, a visual inspection is made, known as the 'walkaround', to check the engines, tire tread and pressure, landing gear, brakes, wings, control surfaces, sensors, and the fuselage. They will look for anything out of the ordinary, such as visible damage that may have been incurred by a bird strike, a bump from loading equipment, leaks, or excessive wear. Although this has to be performed by one of the pilots, it could in theory be done by anyone, as it is the visual asymmetry of damage, leaks, or missing parts that draws the eye.

An hour behind schedule due to weather-related delays in loading the cargo (ramp workers must down tools and retreat to shelter during a lightning strike warning) and airport traffic congestion, we started engines and taxied out for departure for our seven and a half hour flight to Qatar. Weighing over 400 tonnes (nearly 900,000 lbs), we used full power to get airborne and begin our climb to 30,000 feet.

Unlike passenger flights, there are no flight attendants on a freighter. (This meant that the captain gave a safety briefing to us in the passenger area in person!) You simply go to the galley and help yourself, or the loadmaster will assume cooking duties. In my case, it was my first time heating up a meal using the in-flight oven. There were four choices of meal provided by HACTL: beef, chicken, salmon, or pasta. I must say, it didn't look or taste too bad!

The main deck is accessible during flight, with a crawl space along one side of the cargo, but to do so, you must carry an oxygen bottle and mask, in case of

▲ Difficult wing view from an almost-windowless freighter

▲ Spacious seating for commuting pilots and airline employees in the upper deck, aft of the cockpit

a loss of cabin pressure. While I was on the main deck, all the lights started flashing. This happens on the main deck of a freighter when the captain turns on the seatbelt signs, so I returned to the upper deck to get strapped in as we passed through an area of turbulence.

It was an uneventful flight, which routed west across Bangladesh, overhead Calcutta, north of Mumbai, and out across the the Arabian Sea towards the Persian Gulf. At one point we deviated to the north to avoid towering cumulonimbus thunderheads which reached up as high as 45,000 feet. There is no inflight entertainment fitted to freighters as usually only the pilots and a loadmaster are aboard. I took a nap in the crew bunk, and I think that it's actually better than the QSuite on Qatar's passenger fleet.

As soon as we arrived in Doha, just before dusk, cargo offloading activities began immediately. Much of our cargo was transiting onward from Doha; it was transported to Qatar Airways' new flagship cargo facility for temporary storage awaiting onward flight.

The Qatar Airways cargo campus has large dedicated areas including cold storage for perishables (fruit and vegetables, seafood) or pharmaceuticals, a secure area for dangerous goods such as corrosive and flammable items (the most potent of which can only be carried on freighters, not passenger ships), and live animal stations with grooms and vets which routinely handle all manner of exotic creatures including zebras, lions and elephants. Qatar Airways partners with NGOs and have their own humanitarian enterprises, shipping aid to people in need without charge.

Based on IATA's international freight-tonne-kilometre (FTK) rankings, Qatar Airways is one of the world's largest international cargo carriers; as well as the capacious underfloor belly space of its 200+ passenger liners (170 of which are widebodies) which fly to over 90 countries on all six inhabited continents, their 30 dedicated freight aircraft serve over 60 destinations from their Doha hub. Cargo movement mostly happens out of sight of the end user, but almost everything you own, use, or eat has travelled by air, making Qatar Airways a major force in today's global commerce.

▲ Lunch time in the cockpit; crew meals catered on freight flights are generous, close to business class standard

▲ Crew rest is as good as a first class suite!

Two Flights With Saudia 747-300

Saudia is an interesting airline brand – jet equipped for half a century, and seen at most airline hubs of the world. Yet unknown to most – not geared to transit passengers, and dry (no alcohol served onboard). I was always curious to see what they were like.

And it's worth mentioning that Saudia is actually the only airline in the world to have operated every variant of the 747, with the -100B, -200B, SP, -300, -400, and -8F all flying (and in significant quantities). Just when you think no one can love the 747 more than you... ▶

▲ The nose of the jumbo, the most exclusive cabin in the sky

▲ Refreshing fruit juice

▲ Saudia's lunch service started with a soup

Jakarta to Riyadh

A Silver Bird Mercedes provided a very smooth ride from Jakarta's downtown Hotel Indonesia Kempinski to Soekarno-Hatta International airport, where Saudia fly from Terminal 2D, which only serves foreign carriers. Only ticket holders are allowed in the check-in area, where Saudia desks were situated among Cathay Pacific, Jetstar, Emirates and Philippines. The check-in agent was friendly; SV 813 would be leaving ontime at 1300 from gate D6.

With Saudi Arabian airports lacking a transit channel, the handful of transit passengers usually need to be accompanied by an airline agent to get airside for the onward leg. My onward flight from Riyadh to Dubai was on a different carrier – Emirates – necessitating a change of terminal in Riyadh, terminal 2 to terminal 1, and for my documents to be taken ground side in Riyadh to get checked in. Saudia airline officials at Jakarta were worried there wouldn't be an agent available to escort me through the layers of officialdom, and I waited in the Saudia office while clearance was sought, and eventually given, after which I was able to proceed through security and head for the lounge. By the way, Saudia has the biggest presence of any foreign carrier at Jakarta.

The Premier Lounge is a common use premium class lounge and I found it very pleasant – not crowded around noon and offered foot massage and reflexology. The walk to gate D6 was through the Aeroport de Paris-designed terminal with lots of natural light and gently sloping ceilings with lush tropical garden surroundings.

Awaiting us was a sand yellow and royal blue Boeing 747-300, the first 747 to have a stretched upper deck but otherwise a 'minimum-change' variant which retained the original wing, 70s cabin interior and three-crew analogue cockpit. With the mighty 747-400 following right behind, bringing its revolutionary digital systems and new wing denoted by winglets, only 81 747-300s were built, making it a rare subtype and one I was very happy to fly on. (In fact even rarer – Saudia was one of only three airlines alongside Qantas and Cathay Pacific to buy -300s with Roll-Royce engines.)

This particular ship had a great registration, made just for this book: HZ-AIR.

First class was in the nose, and offered big and comfortable La-Z-Boy recliners, with a hot towel and drinks service before takeoff, with an ontime pushback and taxi out to runway two five right. After an impressive takeoff for a fully laden jumbo followed by a climbing curve to the right, setting course for the Arabian Peninsula, eight and a half hours on the nose, west northwest.

The seat was electrically controlled; the leg rest was so generous that the seat almost turned into a bed. Very comfortable to stretch out and relax. At 36,000 feet, the multi-course meal service began, offering Arabic mezze, salad, soup, followed by main courses of chicken, fish, biryani (lamb) and vegetable dishes served onto your plate chairside from the trolley. I had a bit of everything, and found all of it to be delicious. A range of desserts were offered, and I enjoyed a bowl of ice cream and a slice of rich chocolate cake.

After such a fine meal, I requested a bottle of water and to my surprise was given a large two litre bottle. It was the only size they had onboard. A couple of movies were shown on overhead projectors but most passengers were not interested in movies or music.

After a rest, I was invited to tour the aircraft. The upper deck had a high density layout with room for 60 passengers in ten rows of six abreast economy seating, although with only 173 aboard in total, the upper deck was blocked off. On the main deck, the crew showed off an unusual feature found on only a handful of 747s, the sideways galley, most often found on KLM and Thai ships, taking up the righthand side of the cabin between doors one and two.

The pilots were Jeddah based – Captain Al Yamani, First Officer Badjened, and Flight Engineer Buchari – while the cabin crew were Jakarta-based Indonesian nationals. Yup, Saudia's Jakarta flights are so frequent that the route has dedicated cabin crew.

A second meal was served 90 minutes out of Riyadh – chicken pasta, salad and fruit served on one tray. All catering was prepared and loaded in Jakarta. With plates and cups cleared away I enjoyed the last moments of our sunset cruise across the desert before beginning our descent into Riyadh, where we touched down at 17:45 local time, after eight hours and 45 minutes in the air.

After a fond farewell with the crew, King Khalid International was impressively airy, spacious and modern. And in fact a connection to another Saudia flight would be quite straightforward, with departures upstairs, separated from arrivals only by a security check. I was able to do an interline transit. None of this is advertised but it is possible even across different terminals with different airlines.

▲ Saudia's cabin crew in the upper deck, which is all-economy on this people mover

▲ The boarding was slow but I didn't mind at all. It provided more opportunities to take photos like this. Mind you, Jeddah has some of the toughest apron security anywhere. I was lucky they didn't catch me taking photos.

▲ The boarding was slow but I didn't mind at all. It provided more opportunities to take photos like this. Mind you, Jeddah has some of the toughest apron security anywhere. I was lucky they didn't catch me taking photos.

▲ 30 minutes after takeoff, I could see the sunbeams for the first time, reaching out into the clear, dark sky, then ever so slowly pulling level with the horizon before rising above it. It was the most beautiful moment of the day. I enjoyed it so much and couldn't stop taking photos of it.

Jeddah to Khartoum

An incredible adventure to Sudan; this was definitely not for the faint hearted! I chose to fly Saudia again, this time from Dubai to Khartoum. The airfare was good and included stops in Medina and Jeddah. Even better, SV451 from Jeddah to Khartoum gave me another shot at riding on the 747-300.

Boarding by bus and stairs on a remote stand in predawn darkness took nearly an hour, then we closed doors and started engines for our mission to Sudan. For nearly all of the 360 passengers, this was to be a homecoming.

After blasting off out of Saudi Arabia's desert airport, we turned onto a southwesterly course in the climbout over the Red Sea, where we were greeted by an absolutely gorgeous sunrise.

On the western shores of the Red Sea lay Sudan, whose airspace we entered established in the cruise at 35,000 feet. Flight time was an hour and 35 minutes, mostly over the large uninhabited desert of Sudan. Somewhere down there are pyramids dating back to highly technological civilisations that existed thousands of years ago.

During the descent the outskirts the city of Khartoum broke up the monotony of the endless desert. The city proper, sprawled across the two Niles, Blue and White, emerged out of the morning haze right before my eyes. The airport is in the middle of the metropolis; our shadow rippled across the towers and minarets of the city, getting bigger and reaching out towards us. At the last minute, the urban sprawl was replaced by a dividing strip of open land that whipped past for a heartbeat, then the runway was right under us for a smooth touchdown and smudge of tire smoke from under the wings. It was a fabulous early morning run!

Saudia is a humble yet decent airline. It seldom advertises but provided a very solid schedule and product. I was prepared for check in and in flight drama, but the whole operation was mature, and all crew and ground personnel were very experienced. And very happy to have a ride on such a rare Rolls-Royce 747-300. Ahlan Wa Sahlan – welcome aboard!

▲ Breakfast was served with choices of Ful Medames or an omelette. However, the omelette was cold and I think they forgot to heat up the breakfast. The crews were working very fast and served rounds of coffee/tea before landing.

▲ My seatmate, the old man on the left, is 75 years old and on his way back from Hajj. It was his first time. The young man Omar, who was studying in Bangalore, India, and with whom I later became friends, helped me to get access for picture-taking in Khartoum.

▲ The view from the last row of economy class, shortly before landing; You can see the soft sunlight spill through the cabin. We had a load of 360 passengers in total.

Lufthansa First Class On Two Jumbos

Lufthansa has operated the 747 continuously since 1970 and remains an avid supporter of the type, especially now, as one of only three operators worldwide to operate the latest and last passenger variant, the -8i Intercontinental. I am lucky to have flown in first class on both the -400 and the -8i. ▶

The 747-400...

For some years, Lufthansa had a business class product on the 747 that wasn't keeping up with the competition, large reclining seats in pairs more suitable to a mid-range business class than the flagship product of one of the world's premier airline brands.

▲ Lufthansa have a dedicated first class terminal with Mercedes cars for a private airside transfer to the steps of the aircraft

That changed when they introduced their amazing 'one chair and one bed' concept on the upper deck of the 747-400. A generous armchair for takeoff, landing, mealtime, movies and working, and a fully flat bed next to it for relaxing, reading, and sleeping. Philippine Airlines had bunk beds reserved for first class passengers in the upper deck of their jumbos in the 1970s, but nothing like this – where the bed and the seat are separate – has been offered in modern times. I was very keen to fly it!

I was greeted at my seat by a menu with my name handwritten on it – a nice personal touch. Also handed out during boarding were the pyjamas, slippers, and a Rimowa amenity kit. I enjoyed a Mimosa with Macadamia nuts while the other passengers boarded. Only four of us in the upper deck today.

After take off I had a glass of champagne with an amuse bouche, followed by the lavish meal service, which started with caviar, followed by a salad and seafood appetizer, a main course of sea bass with seafood risotto, and finally cheese and dessert.

▲ A view of the upper deck of the 747-400 with the unique 'one chair and one bed' configuration

Our flying time to Dubai was a short six hours 20 minutes. After that very satisfying meal, I climbed into the bed and fell into a deep and relaxing sleep.

One nice feature of the bed is that it is level with the window; you can see the sky view while lying flat. Its location away from the aisle also gives a lot of privacy.

Even though our ontime arrival into Dubai was in the late evening, it was hot and humid outside, in classic Persian Gulf style. The gateway to the orient.

I really enjoyed this product and was sorry that Lufthansa's 747-400s were converted to a two class configuration of just business and economy, so this unique product did not stay long. I am glad I had a chance to fly it while I could!

▲ Lunch started with caviar service, a Lufthansa staple in first class

▲ What a wonderful way to fly!

▲ A salad and seafood appetiser

▲ Main course was sea bass with Indian basmati rice

▲ The 747-400 cockpit after parking and shutdown at the destination, Dubai

...and the 747-8i

Lufthansa was the first airline in the world to order the B747-8 Intercontinental passenger version. In December 2006, the airline ordered 20 of the new jumbo with another 20 as options. It is an ideal fit with Lufthansa's fleet; with 362 seats, the -8i slotted in perfectly between the A340-600 (306 seats) and A380 (526 seats).

Lufthansa is the biggest European airlines serving China. It has the most frequent direct flights between China and Europe. Destinations in China include Beijing, Shanghai, Nanjing, Shenyang, Qingdao and Hong Kong.

Lufthansa and all of the Star Alliance airlines use terminal 3 at Beijing Capital International. As a Star Alliance member, Lufthansa passengers use Air China lounges in Beijing. The lounge has nothing to write home about. Apart from being quite spacious, there were very little food or beverages available.

I turned left from door one to a warm welcome my seat at 1A, the most exclusive address in the sky. At the very front of the plane, there's no engine noise, virtually no foot traffic in the cabin, and feels very exclusive. There's just something about sitting in the nose of the B747. Because of the curvature of the nose, from the windows next to row 1 you can literally see forwards! There is always a cockpit or a galley or a lavatory in front on the B777 or A380, but not on the jumbo.

Lufthansa's first class cabin on the B747-8i is simply stunning, possibly the most elegant of any airline. I'm sure part of it is that the plane is still brand new so it has the 'new car smell' and very little wear and tear, but there's just something so elegant and classy about the minimalist design of Lufthansa's first class cabins. There are only eight first class seats – three along each side by the windows, and two centre seats. This is an extremely generous layout, given that other airlines cram up to 14 first class seats in the nose. The overhead bins and ceiling also received their refreshed new look.

We pushed back on-time with 352 seats occupied out of 362, with three out of eight occupied in first.

▲ To my surprise, I was able to catch some of our condensation trails over a very cold Siberia.

▲ First class cabin ready for passengers

We took off from northerly runway 01 on a relatively clear day in Beijing. After several turns towards the northwest, we crossed a mountain range near Beijing before heading towards Inner Mongolia, then on to Outer Mongolia and Siberia.

About 15 minutes after takeoff, the purser made the rounds for a formal introduction, expressing great pride in their new B747-8i. A lavish lunch was prepared, the catering specially designed by the chefs at the Ritz-Carlton Portman Hotel Shanghai.

After an epic gourmet lunch, I befriended the flight attendants and purser. We exchanged a lot of conversation about what China was like in 1980s vs now. They were all very friendly and did their best to serve their passengers. We took some souvenir photos together. The two ladies serving first class had 26 and 28 years of experience, respectively. We landed in the

▲ Generous seat and a nice cabin atmosphere for Lufthansa's most high-value customers

late afternoon at Frankfurt after nine hours and 44 minutes in the air, chasing the sun all day across the roof of the world.

So how does the latest Queen Of The Skies compare with the A380? The A380 and 747-8i are both great aircraft with their own benefits. Both feature double deck seating. In a beauty contest, hands down, the 747-8i takes the crown. I have not heard one single 'ugly 747' comment yet. The A380 is an aviation marvel that functions well, but it doesn't have the grace or history that the 747 has. In the noise and size department, I think the A380 is superb to fly with. To me, the most outstanding differentiating factor between the two is the B747's nose area. It is truly an exclusive area confined to only few lucky passengers with literally nothing in front of you!

I enjoyed tremendously my first 747-8i flight. The Intercontinental is not only a beautiful aircraft, but one that flies very well. With my usual enthusiasm and positive attitude, the flight is flawless. Lufthansa is my favourite European airline because they deliver a consistent level of professional service with elegance and sophistication. They are well-known for quality, ingenuity and reliability. No doubt, the 747-8i is the latest chapter in the love affair between Lufthansa and the 747, one of the most enduring partnerships in aviation history.

▲ For main, there were four choices, I chose scallops with Chinese XO sauce and rice.

▲ Cheese and dessert cart.

▲ Trio of appetizers: smoked duck breast, prawns and grilled vegetable with salad.

▲ With first class cabin crew

▲ 747-8i cockpit is almost the same as the 747-400, so pilots can fly both without any extra training

▲ Spacious first class washrooms include a bench to sit on while changing, and even a window

▲ First class seat in bed mode. Perfect for a deep and restful sleep at 35,000 feet

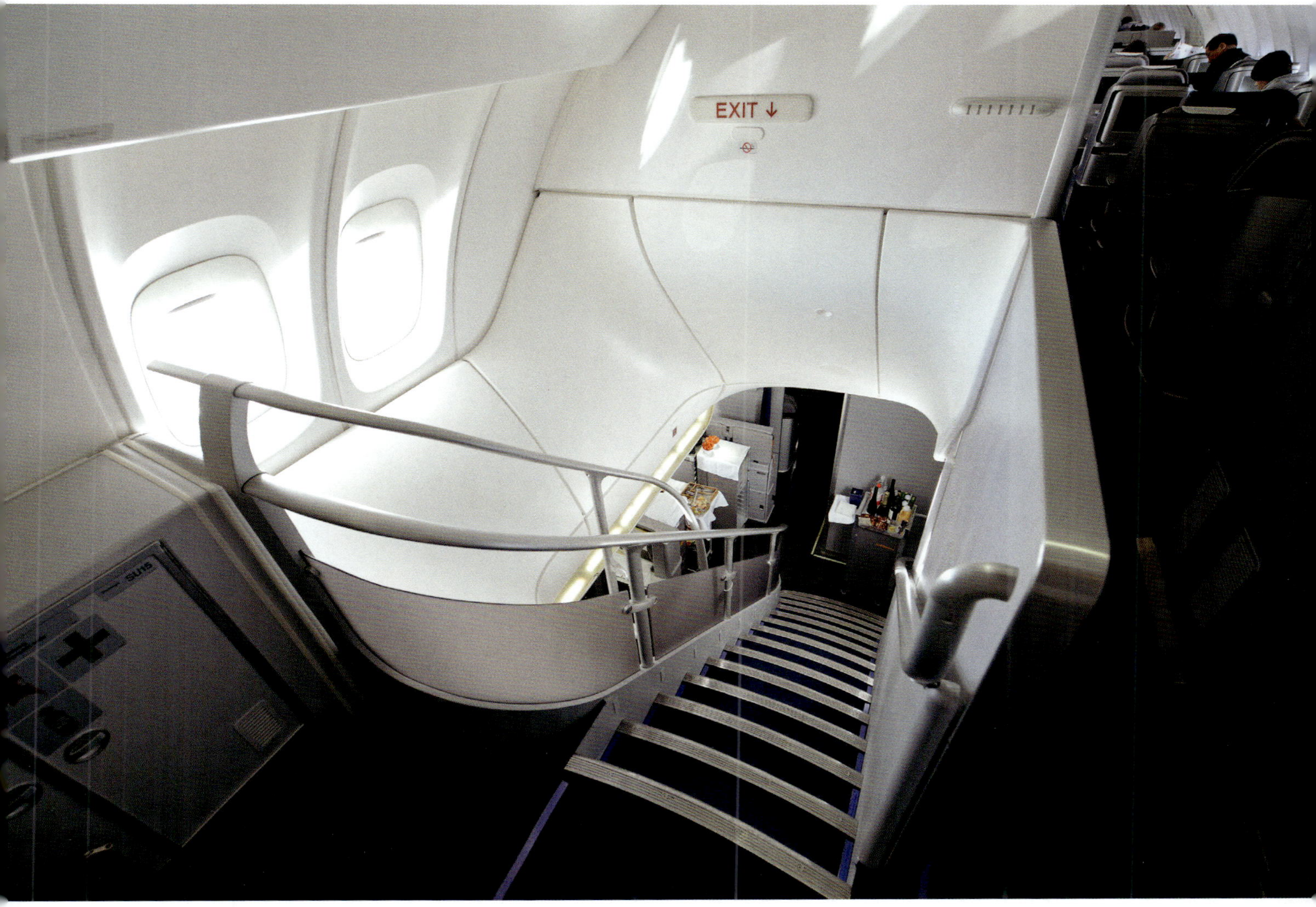

▲ New cabin architecture on the 747-8i including a new design for the stairs down to the main deck

▲ Entrance, service area, meeting place

▲ Upper deck business class

Orient Thai was a Bangkok-based independent carrier, operating a very cosmopolitan fleet of secondhand 747s acquired from a variety of sources. The fleet included all of the traditional subtypes, including four -100s, nine -200Bs, seven -300s, and four -400s. Two of the -100s were rare SUD models, short for Stretched Upper Deck, meaning a major mid life structural addition to have the upper deck of the -300 or -400. These, like a lot of the

▲ The beauty of Thai waterways and the majesty of a classic Boeing

▲ Orient Thai's cosmopolitan fleet of secondhand jumbos came from all over the world. This -300 was originally delivered to KLM way back in 1984

fleet (and 767-300s too) were acquired from Japan Airlines, one of only two airlines (the other being KLM) to make this major investment in their old Classics. Other Orient Thai 747s came from Qantas, Singapore Airlines, Canadian Pacific, and Korean Air.

The airline was founded in 1995 by Thai entrepreneur Udom Tantiprasonchai. Thanks to his close personal links to the Thai king Rama IX, it was the only airline besides the national carrier to bear a royal seal. Orient Thai was a leisure airline, dedicated to flying tourists in from other parts of Asia, most notably Japan, and the provincial cities of China. Their 747s were configured with high density seating throughout the main deck, making them one of the few airlines to have economy seating in the nose, usually reserved for first class on airlines that targeted a mix of business and tourist traffic.

The parent company owned a separate airline brand, One-Two-GO, for domestic services within Thailand. Some of the Orient Thai 747 fleet passed through the ranks of One-Two-GO, making it possible for a fan of vintage jumbos to fly on a 747-100, a -200B or a -300 for $40 to Chiang Mai or Phuket from Bangkok, in the years between the creation of the brand in 2003 until around 2007 when One-Two-GO standardised on the narrowbody McDonnell Douglas MD-80 instead. The brand was merged with Orient Thai in 2010.

Routes to China and Japan came and went, and many were only bookable as part of a holiday package, but the daily trunk route to Hong Kong was easier to book, albeit on days with a light load, a 767 or even, occasionally, a narrowbody (737 or MD-80) took the place of the jumbo.

The airline operated until ceasing flight operations in July 2018 and the company liquidating in October of the same year. They had a patchy reputation with regulators both at home and in Japan (due to a navigation error, one of their -200Bs missed the Eiffel Tower-inspired Tokyo Tower by just 500 feet) but from an enthusiasts point of view Orient Thai were a fascinating operator, and one of the very select group of airlines to have operated the -100, -200B, -300 and -400.

▲ This ex Japan Airlines 747-100 cabin is still in perfect condition despite its age

▲ Old fashioned business class in the upper deck

▲ The analogue cockpit of the 747 Classic

History Special: British Airways 747

British Airways was formed by the 1972 merger of Britain's two state-owned flag carriers — BEA (British European Airways) which covered short and medium haul trips with an entirely British-built fleet of Tridents, BAC-111s, Viscounts and Vanguards, and BOAC (British Overseas Airways Corporation) which flew intercontinental with a fleet of British-built VC-10s and American Boeing 707s.

BOAC were considering all options including the stretched Douglas DC-8-63 and Vickers' homegrown Super-Super VC-10, a reimagined Super VC-10 that never left the drawing board. Factors that influenced BOAC towards the Boeing 747 were the obvious savings to be achieved by flying 370 people in a single aeroplane, and a shortage of pilots that was expected to last into the foreseeable future.

In April 1966, BOAC purchased six Boeing 747s; as performance forecasts from Boeing became more concrete as the 747 design neared completion, the true scale of the efficiencies that could be realised by operating such a large and modern machine that the board soon placed a follow-up order for another ten planes, with 20 percent of the purchase to be financed by BOAC's ticket sales in the US which were in dollars.

Around the time of 747 deliveries were intended to begin, it was realized that a long-running pay dispute with pilots would endanger summer 1970 flying. The airline's labour problems soon multiplied as flight engineers insisted on retaining their two-night stopover privileges, and cabin crew wanted extra "747 pay" — and compensation for crew who weren't selected to work on the jumbo. Pilots refused to start training until the disputes were settled.

The first jumbo for BOAC and the twenty-third built was G-AWNA, flown into London Heathrow on April 22, 1970, followed by G-AWNB on May 6 and G-AWNC on May 28. The machines were parked and stored while the dispute rumbled on. In fact this saved BOAC a considerable headache, as the early Pratt & Whitney JT9D engines on the 747-100 were extremely unreliable in service (the first ever 747 passenger flight, Pan Am's inaugural New York to London trip on January 6, 1970, was delayed by nearly ten hours including an eventual aircraft change). BOAC was able to bypass these teething problems while its labour problems were ironed out, even leasing some of their engine inventory to other airlines who desperately needed them as their own spares were rapidly exhausted.

It wasn't until early 1971 when contracts with pilots and cabin crew were settled and all nominated staff reported for training on March 1, with 747s getting airborne on passenger services on April 14. The inaugural flight was to New York JFK operated by G-AWNF departing Heathrow at 1203 under the command of BOAC's 747 Flight Manager Captain D. Redrup. Initially the frequency was twice weekly, reaching daily the following month. Within a year the 747 fleet was flying daily to Chicago and Miami, followed by Montreal, Bermuda and Toronto. Summer 1972 also included a Manchester-Prestwick-New York service.

The cabin layout was for 27 first class passengers and 335 in economy; in winter the configuration was changed to 36 first class and 315 in economy. First class passengers also had the use of the Monarch Lounge in the upper deck, accessed by a spiral staircase and containing a luxurious hide-out for 16 passengers to enjoy the services of a bartender and relax on settees and couches. ▶

(photo by Catarina Madueira)

Although the merger with BEA was not formalised until March 31, 1974, the last 747-136 delivered in BOAC livery was G-AWNM which arrived at Heathrow on May 3, 1973. G-AWNN onwards were delivered in British Airways livery in anticipation of the merger. The last 747-136 to be delivered was G-BDPV on April 4, 1976, by which time the jumbo was flying throughout the network including the bulk of transatlantic trips, across the pole to Japan, and all Australia and New Zealand routes.

Rolls-Royce had created the RB.211 high-bypass turbofan for Lockheed's L-1011 Tristar, a development so ambitious that it bankrupted Rolls, which survived only by being nationalised by the British government. Political pressure to make the taxpayer's investment profitable may have been a factor for government-owned British Airways' order for RB.211-powered 747-200Bs, but in any case the engine, with its unique triple-stage fan, was a world-beater. The prototype for Rolls-powered 747s, which were also ordered by Qantas, Cathay Pacific, Air New Zealand, Malaysia, and Saudia, was G-BDXA, which began test flying in September 1976. One memorable test flight saw 'XA lift off at a weight of 381.25 tonnes, at that time the heaviest aircraft in history.

One 747-236F pure freighter was delivered in October 1980, intended to be G-BDXK but aptly registered G-KILO. However, the economy in the early 1980s was soft, and it was decided that the passenger 747 fleet had ample underfloor cargo capacity, so it was sold to Cathay Pacific in March 1982 (where it received another custom registration, VR-HVY).

On the night of June 24, 1982, G-BDXH made history as the world's heaviest glider when it flew without engine power for 12 minutes after flying into an unforecast cloud of volcanic ash over Indonesia. Luckily three of the engines were restarted after the machine glided clear of the ash cloud and a challenging but safe landing was achieved by ace pilot Captain Eric Moody and his crew at Jakarta.

The final 747-236Bs were delivered in the 1987-1988 period, a trio with main deck side cargo doors, although they were never used as combis. Interestingly, Boeing were already manufacturing the horizontal stabilizer for the 747-400 which included integral fuel tanks, so although they were never plumbed in with fuel pumps, those ships had -400 stabilisers.

British Airways was one of the first airlines to place an order for the 747-400, with an initial order for 16 aircraft announced on August 16, 1986. As with the -200B, was the first airline to receive aircraft powered by Rolls-Royce engines. G-BNLA and 'LB were handed over to their new owner on June 30, 1989. The inaugural flight of the 747-400 in British Airways service took place on Thursday July 27, with Speedbird 219 pushing back from Terminal 4 at Heathrow at 1232 local time bound for Philadelphia, where it landed at 1520 local time, before continuing on for the short hop to Pittsburgh where it landed at 1750.

A week later, the 747-400 took over the trip to Detroit via Montreal. The multistop flights were favoured initially, as the extra sectors allowed more takeoffs and landings, giving crew more opportunities to get type rated on the airline's new flagship. The extra range of the -400 was used to its full extent on ultra longhaul nonstops to Singapore, Tokyo, Sao Paolo, and Johannesburg, displacing the Classics which retreated to shorter trips such as Toronto, New York, Washington, the Persian Gulf, and India.

A new livery was introduced in 1997, known as the Utopia scheme, and was an innovative reflection of the wide range of global destinations served by British Airways, and included 12 different tail designs based on ethnic art from every corner of the world. While colourful and unique, some elements of the airline's core customer base felt it diluted the "Britishness" of the brand, and the tail design that had been created just for Concorde, a stylised Union flag known as the Chatham Historic Dockyard was adopted fleet-wide in 1999.

The only 747-200 to receive the Chatham Historic Dockyard livery was G-BDXB, as the Classics were coming up to retirement. The first to leave the fleet was BOAC's first 747-136, G-AWNA, which was exited from the fleet in Nov 1998; to mark the occasion, she was painted in a basic BOAC livery for final weeks of service before being ferried to Bruntingthorpe and scrapped.

The last Classic to leave the fleet was a -236B, flying from Bombay to London on the last day of October 2001, the retirement plans hastened by the post 9/11 downtown in air traffic.

In topping up orders for more of the 747-400, British Airways requested a unique variant, known as the 747 Lite. By not plumbing in some of the auxiliary fuel tanks, the 747-400 Lite was recertified with a lower maximum takeoff weight, from 396,900 kg down to 381,000 kg, increasing payload by 6,000 kg and still paying lower landing fees and overflight fees. The only visible difference on these ships is found in the cockpit, where two fuel tank switches are replaced by a blank panel.

Further top-ups had raised the size of the 747-436 fleet to 50, yet British Airways had plans for a total of 75. The final 25 – representing an order for a further 100 engines – were to be powered by a special hybrid of the RB.211, utilizing the core from the Trent engine. However, only nine of this final order were built before British Airways decided 59 jumbos was enough, and deposits for the rest of the order were transferred to Trent-powered 777-236ERs. Interestingly, today those unique RB.211s with the Trent core, over the years of engine changes between ships, turn up randomly on various British Airways 747s. With the sophisticated FADEC engine management software, they produce identical thrust to the rest of the engine pool, but are notable in flight because they burn slightly less fuel and run with slightly lower exhaust gas temperatures (EGTs), which is usually the only way operating crew will notice they have one of those engines along for the ride.

As well as innovating with technology, British Airways has always been at the cutting edge of passenger accommodation; in May 1977 it was one of the first airlines to introduce business class, starting with the 747. The new cabin was called Executive Class (incidentally the origin of BA's frequent flier programme which is called the Executive Club to this day), renamed Super Club in March 1981 on US routes and extended to the rest of the long haul network in 1984, and relaunched as Club World in 1987.

British Airways stunned the airline world with a revolutionary move in March 2000 by introducing flat beds in Club World, the first flat bed in business class on any airline. World Traveller Plus, a premium economy product, was launched on November 11, 2000, an innovation initially created by Eva Air of Taiwan (Evergreen Class).

Three 747-400Fs were operated between 1999 and 2001 on behalf of British Airways World Cargo by Global Supply Systems, a British company based at Stansted; of the three (N491MC, N494MC and N495MC), the latter was painted in the Utopia Chelsea Rose livery. In November 2011 the arrangement was resurrected when three 747-8Fs were put on the British register as G-GSSD, SE and SF and painted in full BA livery. Alas the operation was not a lasting success and in May 2014 the three were returned to Atlas Air; there are likely to be the only 747-8s that are ever seen in BA livery.

Even as the oldest -400s were stood down, the decades-long love affair continued at the World's Favourite Airline — as Bloomberg put it, "British Airways Just Can't Kick Its 747 Habit". A new subfleet was created for routes with high business class demand, with the main deck Club World cabin extending all the way to the trailing edge of the wing, with a total of 86 Club World seats, leaving only a single economy (World Traveller) cabin at the rear of the main deck with 143 seats — the same as on all-economy Airbus A319.

The 747 was displaced from some of its signature routes by the larger Airbus A380, and the more efficient Boeing 777, but up until the coronavirus grounding, remained a stronghold on the 'Blue Ribband' New York route with multiple daily trips as well as schedules to Accra, Boston, Cape Town, Chicago, Dallas, Delhi, Dubai, Houston, Kuwait, Lagos, Las Vegas, Miami, Riyadh, Sao Paolo, Toronto, and Vancouver. For 50 years, British Airways and the 747 have been a match made in heaven. All good things must come to an end, but this was a partnership to remember.

British Airways' Speedbird 747

▲ The spacious main deck business class cabin

▲ Speedbird 268 pushes back and calls for taxi

British Airways stunned the world by introducing the world's first flat bed in business class in 2000. Many predicted this would hurt British Airways – why would anyone fly in first? Well there is plenty of room for additional luxury to be provided beyond a flat bed, as we have seen in the years since, with airlines like Singapore and Emirates raising the stakes by walling off their first class passengers in completely private suites.

The Club World product had a refresh in 2006 which replaced a fabric-and-wood patina with lighter and more durable plastics, but the layout and proportions remained basically unchanged. It was such a revolutionary leap forward that it left every other business class product behind for years. Perhaps this bred complacency in British Airways. Other airlines, most notably Air New Zealand, Air Canada and Virgin Atlantic, had a false start with the so-called herringbone layout, a less-than-ideal configuration which did manage to introduce a flat bed (at 45 degrees to the direction of travel) but with no eye contact with other passengers, making it unfriendly for couples or families, and put the window effectively out of reach behind the passenger. But the idea of flat beds running diagonally led to the improved reverse-herringbone layout, with more room, more privacy, a window-facing aspect, and centre pairs that face each other for travel companions who prefer company to solace.

Today, British Airways' yin-and-yang Club World layout has, two decades after it was introduced, become outdated, and with the introduction of the Airbus A350, British Airways unveiled a new Club World product, a surprisingly ordinary off-the-shelf reverse-herringbone seat which will please those on social media who claim to hate the classic yin-and-yang, although shows little of the innovation that the airline demonstrated when they broke the mould 20 years ago.

To experience the classic product, I flew with the airline from Los Angeles. After a typical British Airways welcome – casual but friendly – I settled into my rear-facing window seat. Not only does flying backwards take absolutely no time at all to get used to, but for an enthusiast, gives a rare view that is hard to find elsewhere, looking rearwards, of the wing, drooping with the weight

▲ I used the Private Suite ground product at LAX which includes a personalised car transfer from the VIP terminal to the aircraft

▲ Rearward-facing middle seats for couples

of all the fuel needed for the long flight to London, and looking directly into the engines (which are Rolls-Royce Trents, only ever installed on 747s of British Airways, Qantas, Cathay Pacific and Air New Zealand).

We climbed out through a thin so-called 'marine layer' of fog into the evening sunshine, and, after a sweeping right turn, heading northeast towards Nevada, Idaho, Montana, and Canada on our Great Circle track on the polar route to London. I went to the galley at the invitation of the cabin crew, and chatted about how much they love the 747. "We call it the Queen Of The Skies," they told me. "747 – it epitomises mass travel. This is the way to travel. We try to make all our guests feel special, from newborn babies to the most frequent flier, and for us, it's a total honour to be on this plane. Such a solid workhorse for us. The crew love them, our customers love them as well."

▲ Rare roast beef appetiser

▲ A main course of gnocci with salmon

The classic British Airways Club World flat bed product is configured in pairs, with one wide seat facing one way next to the legs of the other passenger who flies backwards. One drawback is that during takeoff and landing, the privacy screen between the two seats is lowered, so you are, albeit an angle, facing a stranger. Also, the high density achieved leaves almost no storage space beyond a small drawer under the feet.

A small advantage compared to the reverse herringbone is there is nothing above your feet, which are not in a footwell underneath the seat in front of you, and a major advantage in non-aisle seats, which is that once that privacy divider goes up, you have complete privacy, comparable to one of those Emirates or Singapore first class suites. The 747 I was flying on was one of the subfleet of low density machines with 86 business class seats – 20 in the upper deck and 66 on the main deck, stretching all the way back to the trailing edge of the wing, leaving just 14 rows of economy in the rearmost cabin. This flight was not full, so I could try different seats. The aisle seats face forward, and the middle pairs face rearwards.

Dinner was not bad, a rare roast beef starter, and a gnocci with salmon main. British Airways, who have never been famous for their food, have definitely improved their premium cabin offering in recent years, with catering provided by Do & Co, and upgraded bedding from the White Company, which includes a comforter and an extra blanket. I slept well for five hours, waking up with just 90 minutes remaining to London. The crew brought me a classic English mixed grill breakfast, which I enjoyed with a cup of tea and that beautiful wing-and-engine view.

After a soft touchdown by British Airways' famously skilled pilots, I was thanked by the friendly (albeit camera-shy) crew for flying 747, and disembarked into Heathrow's terminal 5 and headed for the British Airways arrivals lounge, an impressive facility for their many premium cabin transit passengers to freshen up with a shower and enjoy the generous breakfast spread, including an English staple, black pudding. I was grateful for the opportunity to get a massage to combat the jetlag and prepare me for my onward journey. It was a great transatlantic trip, and nice to fly with an airline that clearly love the jumbo as much as I do.

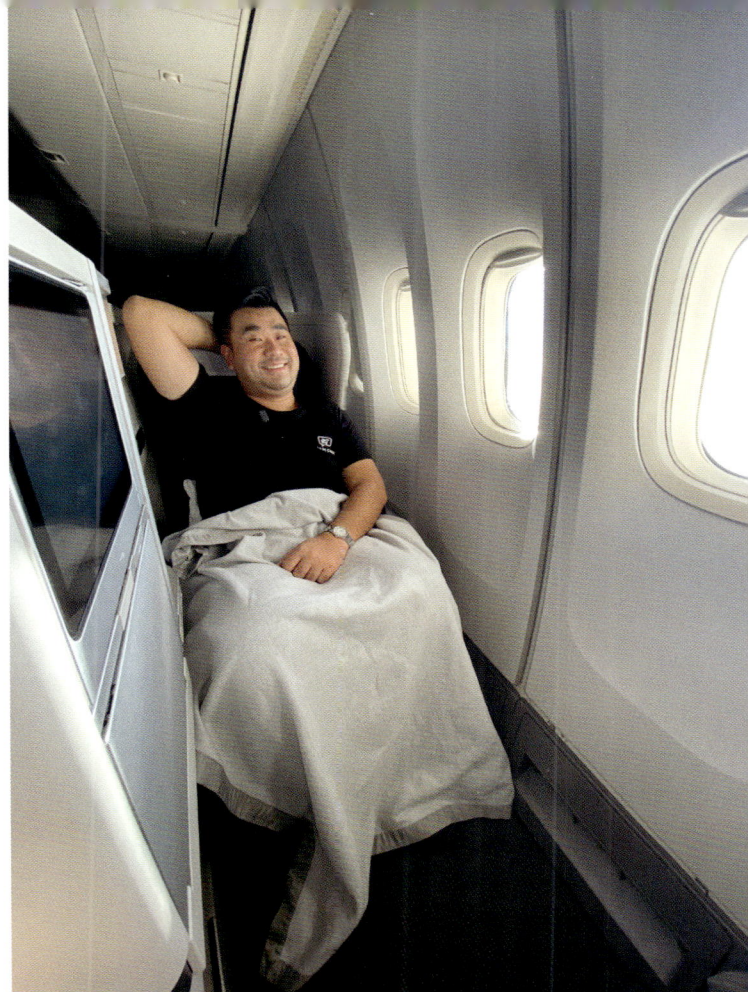

▲ Always happy flying 747!

▲ Classic cooked English breakfast before landing

Qantas And The 747: A Tribute

Of all the 747 retirements, there was never going to be one as significant as Qantas. Celebrating its centenary this year, Qantas have been flying internationally since before World War Two, and was operating round the world (by flying to London via Asia/Europe, and via the Pacific, San Francisco and New York) with 707s by 1959 (the transatlantic leg ended in the early 1970s). But the fares were out of the reach of everyone but captains of industry, movie stars, diplomats. Everyone else went by ship until the dawning of the age of the jumbo.

When Qantas' first 747-238B was delivered to Sydney 1971, it plugged Australia, the most distant of all continents, into the world map at last. Generations of Australians' big overseas trip was on a Qantas 747, discovering neighbouring Asia and turning Singapore and Hong Kong into Aussie cities by association. Double decker bus tours of Europe, getting drunk in Munich, getting high in Amsterdam. And in London, Earls Court became known to Aussies and locals alike as Kangaroo Valley. Later, Australia's cultural focus widened to include California. All of this was possible because of the 747.

Qantas' first 747-400, nicknamed Longreach (not only for the range of the new bird but Qantas' founding town in remote outback Queensland), flew the then-world's longest flight, from London to Sydney, on August 17, 1988, arriving over the harbour with a couple of hours of fuel still on tap. Farewell o'dark-thirty fuel stops in the Persian Gulf, hello 14-hour nonstop sectors such as Singapore to London and Sydney to Los Angeles.

The last Qantas 747 flight to London was in 2010, and to California, San Francisco in early December 2019, squeezed out by the A380 and B787. After that, the Queen Of The Skies was supposed to enjoy an 18 month victory lap on the Johannesburg, Tokyo and Santiago runs, followed by the biggest farewell party the aviation world has ever seen.

Alas, the toll of coronavirus Covid-19 has brought a halt to almost all air traffic worldwide, with a recovery expected to last years. When global mass transit kickstarts, however, one of the great combinations, Qantas and the 747, will be missing at Kingsford-Smith and destinations on three other continents.

The last Qantas 747 flight was QF 28 operated by VH-OEE, from Santiago to Sydney, landing at 1730 Sydney time on Sunday, March 29, 2020, with a series of wide sweeping turns over the famous harbour and skyline of Australia's global city, saying farewell to the nation she served so faithfully.

▲ Qantas' unique 747-400ERs had the cabin architecture of the 777

▲ Two hardworking Qantas 747-338s at the airline's Sydney base, one coming in to land at the end of a long flight while another sets sail for distant shores

▲   Qantas have painted several planes in special liveries created by Aboriginal-owned, Sydney-based Balarinji design studio, including two of the best looking jumbos ever. Nalanji Dreaming (top) was a celebration of the balance and harmony of nature in Australia, reflecting the lush colour palette of tropical Australia, and Wunala Dreaming (bottom) was inspired by the bright reds of Central Australia, the purple-blues of desert mountain ranges, and the lush greens of tropical Kakadu National Park.

The Last United 747

▲ With the crew, and two paintings of United I commissioned from a Hong Kong artist back in the 90s

My love for aviation began with a flight from Hong Kong to Tokyo Narita aboard United flight 800, a brand-new 747-400, in 1993. Since that day I have flown over 70 transpacifics aboard United 747s, including my first international business class flight and my first international first class flight.

United began operating the 747 in June 1970, more than a decade before it had any international route authority. Those big 747-100s were strictly for heavy lift transcontinental trips like New York to Los Angeles, and for a market that United ruled without equal: Hawaii. The 80s saw the opening of flights to Asia, beginning with a solitary Seattle to Tokyo route, but the trickle became a flood in 1985 when United bought Pan Am's entire Pacific network for $250 million (today a billion). From multiple gateways across the USA, United became the dominant carrier overnight to Japan, the Philippines, Hong Kong, Singapore, Thailand, Australia and New Zealand. This massive expansion triggered a buying spree, the then-biggest order ever placed with Boeing, which included 52 of the new generation 747-400. The new variant's extra range made it perfect for long overwater stretches, and enormous passenger- and cargo-carrying ability came just in time to meet the booming Asian market.

▲ Takeoff performance data including runway, weight, flap settings, thrust settings and speeds. At 166 knots, the captain will raise the nose and we will lift into the air.

Yet after decades of service, the 747s were getting old and ready for replacement, mostly by big twins like the 777. United was down to a fleet of 20 at the start of 2017, and the retirement plans were announced soon after. The summer schedule saw the end of Chicago flying by the 747, leaving only San Francisco, with flights to Tokyo, Hong Kong, Seoul, Shanghai, Beijing, London, and Frankfurt. And the last ever flight was scheduled: Seoul to San Francisco, on October 29.

I positioned to Seoul from Dubai via Bangkok. I was very excited about the trip yet so anxious that I didn't sleep well the night before. I arrived at check-in more than three hours before departure time, and only visited the Asiana lounge for about 20 minutes before heading to the gate to see the big ship coming in from San Francisco around three p.m.

United hosted a small ceremony at the gate to commemorate their last 747 flight. Country manager David Ruch gave a farewell speech to the Queen of the Sky. There were a lot of aviation enthusiasts present for the flight, including sold out first and business class cabins. As a result of the demand, there were over 20 Mileage Plus 1Ks and a Global Service card holder – United's top tier frequent fliers – travelling in economy as a result of the sold out premium cabins.

Boarding took longer than usual because of the number of enthusiasts taking pictures from every angle. Onboard, we found that United had placed a last flight

▲ The spacious cabin of the 747 ensures a comfortable and spacious ride even in economy.

▲ Main deck business class.

▲ United curated a specially themed amenity kit for premium cabin passengers in the final month of 747 service.

certificate on every seat (in a cardboard envelope in economy; in a smart wooden frame in business and first). The business class amenity kit was 747 themed, not only on the outer metal tin but also the eyeshades, and included 747-themed aircraft trading cards.

We took off from Incheon's runway three-three, accompanied by a beautiful view from the setting sun. After circling the field in a climbing turn, we set course for the east, towards Japan and the Pacific.

The appetizer was a trio of tuna ahi; for my main course I had the Korean style Bulgogi beef. The highlight of the meal was the fully-loaded dessert cart. Everyone loves an ice cream sundae!

After the last of the dinner service was cleared away, I changed into the pyjamas provided and went to explore the aircraft and discuss our passion with fellow enthusiasts. The crew were also very hospitable and shared their memories of flying on the 747. I brought with me two paintings of United 747s at Kai Tak by Dutch artist Mario Van Eeren and the whole crew signed the frames. I was able to send my log book up to the flight deck; the pilots gave me a copy of the flight plan and a map as a gift. I did not sleep for a minute, I did not even recline my seat for a single minute. I was having such an amazing time over the Pacific!

Breakfast was served ninety minutes prior to landing in San Francisco; choices were Korean noodles, fruit plate or egg frittata. With only the final minutes of the flight remaining, I took more photos as I tried to savour every last second onboard. By 10:45am we were on approach to San Francisco, which was covered by a marine layer of morning fog. The landing was one of the smoothest ever, and a heartfelt round of applause rose in harmony with the roar of reverse thrust. "All hail the queen, long live the queen!" said the captain on the PA as we taxied in to the gate.

With no onward flight to operate, the ground crew were in no rush to get us off, and so there was a long round of group photos and cockpit visits before it was finally time to say goodbye. Time marches on, but the 747 was an icon for United.

▲ Mission accomplished as I shake hands with the captain after arriving at the gate in San Francisco.

▲ The cabin crew, still looking fresh after a long transpacific flight, assemble in the first class cabin for one last group photo before saying goodbye to the 747.

Singapore Airlines 747-400 Farewell

▲ The party started even before boarding

Singapore Airlines joined the 747 club in 1973, with nearly 100 ships passing through the ranks. With its extended upper deck, Singapore nicknamed the -300 the Big Top, and the -400 most famously the Megatop. However, with the advent of Singapore's launch order for the Airbus A380 and a huge fleet of 777 twins, the 747's time with Singapore was finally starting to run out, and a retirement flight was announced for Friday, April 6, 2012.

SQ 747 was the flight number for the morning's outbound leg to Hong Kong, returning to home base for the last time as SQ 748. Check-in was a hive of activity, with portraits of Singapore 747s hanging in between digital screens directing passengers to their counters. All were invited to the party at gate 25, where cake and drinks were served and passengers posed for photos with Singapore Girl flight attendants. Speeches were made, including by the airline's vice-president, and a dance off was held, featuring every era of Singapore Airlines' existence, going back to the early 70s.

The 747 assigned to the trip, 9V-SPQ, was delivered new from the Boeing factory in Seattle on the last day of October 2001, and was now ready for her final mission for the airline. Boarding commenced for the 337 passengers at 2:15pm and I had two empty seats next to me in row 66. Flight attendant Magladene Tay took the aisle seat, as extra crew were working this special trip, and all the jump seats were occupied.

Once airborne, the party started, with passengers moving freely around the aircraft, snapping pictures, making new friendships and renewing old ones. A brief calm followed as everyone took their seats for the meal service (in economy, fried fish or steak, with a commemorative cake).

When the big jet touched down at Singapore's Changi airport in the purple light of dusk, the cabin erupted in cheers. On the taxi in to the gate, there was a special PA announcement commemorating the occasion. "For many of you passengers, it is through these 747 aircraft that the love for commercial aircraft began. And for Singapore staff and crew, this was the aircraft in which most of us grew up in."

An emotional and historic day to say goodbye to one of the most definitive 747 operators, and I am glad I was able to be a part of it.

▲ Plenty of aviation enthusiasts turned out for this special flight

▲ A toast to the Queen Of The Skies

▲ Singapore Girls love the 747!

▲ Even the caterers got involved

▲ Isabelle Chu on the right is a big SQ fan and was also on the A380 inaugural to Sydney

Last Flight Of El Al's 747

After 48 years of service, El Al retired their last 747 in November 2019 with a special flight from the Israeli capital of Tel Aviv to Rome and back. A seat on one of these flights were only available for El Al's Matmid frequent flyer programme members. A roundtrip on the last 747-400 flight cost 747 Matmid Points in Business Class or 400 Matmid Points in Economy Class. The seats were sold out within days. I was invited as media. In fact, I think I was the only non-Jewish and non-Israeli passenger! El Al's 747-400 configuration was 55 Business Class seats (including eight old first class seats sold as business) and 348 Economy Class seats, for a total of 403 seats.

For the Tel Aviv to Rome leg, there was a Goodbye 747 sign on most of the check-in desks. A reception was held at the gate which displayed a lot of El Al 747 pictures and unforgettable moments, most notably 1991's Operation Solomon, which evacuated 14,325 Ethiopian Jews to settle in Israel, including one 747 flight which airlifted over 1,100 people, a record to this day.

The flight was definitely an unusual one, with flight attendants welcoming guests while dressed in

Farewell 747 T-shirts (I was later given one of these to celebrate the occasion). Our flight was operated by Captain Maoz Tsur and First Officer Ayal Perry, aboard 4X-ELC. Flight time to Rome was three hours cruising over the Mediterranean at 36,000 feet. Many of the 18 crew who operated this flight were family, including the two pursers who are husband and wife; the captain's daughter was also a flight attendant.

The economy class meal included a choice of omelette or blintzes (pancakes with sweet cheese), while business class meals included egg shakshuka or fried rosti vegetables.

The flight deck was open to visitors during the flight. Who would've thought that the world's most secure airline would allow this? Special occasion! After three hours, we landed on runway 16R at Rome Fiumicino (FCO). We received a water cannon salute before taxing to the gate. It was Captain Maoz Tsur's last landing on the 747, and was a perfect landing!

After two days weekending in Rome (in accordance with Jewish custom, El Al does not fly on the sabbath, Saturday), on Sunday it was time to fly the last ever El Al 747 flight back to Tel Aviv. El Al were making sure that this flight would be extra special! ▶

▲ Plentiful signage at the gate

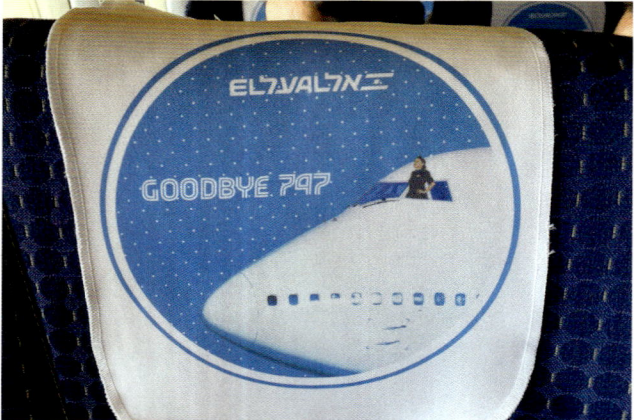

▲ Special headrests for a special flight

▲ El Al produced a series of first day covers, which airlines used to do in the days when air mail was an innovation

There was another gate ceremony, with flight attendants dressed in retro uniforms (circa 1970s). This flight was commanded by El Al's 747 fleet manager, Captain Jonathan Gat, joined by first officer Ayal Perry. We departed 30 minutes late and were finally airborne off runway 25 around 11:10 local time.

We carried a total of 434 persons including extra crew and their families. Every seat, including every jumpseat and crew rest, was occupied, as so many staff and friends wanted to bid a farewell to the 747.

On this flight, there were special bartenders serving cocktails to all passengers, with lunch consisting of lasagne or cannelloni. Special farewell 747 chocolates and tiramisu were handed out to all. I enjoyed my lunch inside the best office, the cockpit at 35,000 ft. Other

▲ Cabin crew in vintage 1970s-style uniforms

▲ Business class on the upper deck; not the most modern product but perfectly comfortable for a red eye from Tel Aviv to New York, which was the flagship route for El Al's 747-400 fleet

▲ Every seat on our celebratory flight was occupied

▲ Leading edge slats deploy as we descend over the Mediterranean inbound to Tel Aviv

passengers were also allowed to visit the cockpit during the flight.

After 90 minutes, we descended to 10,000 feet to perform a very special detail, creating the outline of a Boeing 747 with our flightpath. The idea was from El Al's marketing department, and was planned by the flight department. Over 80 additional way points were entered into FMC (flight management computer) to ensure the drawing would be precise.

The speed of the plane was reduced to between 180 and 200 knots during the drawing to ensure that it could turn slowly and precisely. It took nearly two hours to complete the complex drawing. Thousands of people around the world followed our progress on FlightRadar24 and other tracking apps. We received flight messages from EL AL that said, you're looking good, the [outline of the] engines is perfect. The cabin was quiet during this special activity as the plane was doing many turns at various speeds. Most passengers were seated and strapped in, but many took to looking out of the window. The captain increased speed during straight line travel but had to reduce speed during turns, to make sure our drawing retained its the correct shape.

After we completed the drawing, the entire cabin erupted with cheers and joy. We climbed back to 31,000 feet and continued our remaining journey into Tel Aviv. Before the end of the flight every passenger was presented with retro postcards, including a flight certificate.

El Al made an impressive effort to bid farewell to the 747 in a unique way, and I salute them for this. Shalom! 💬

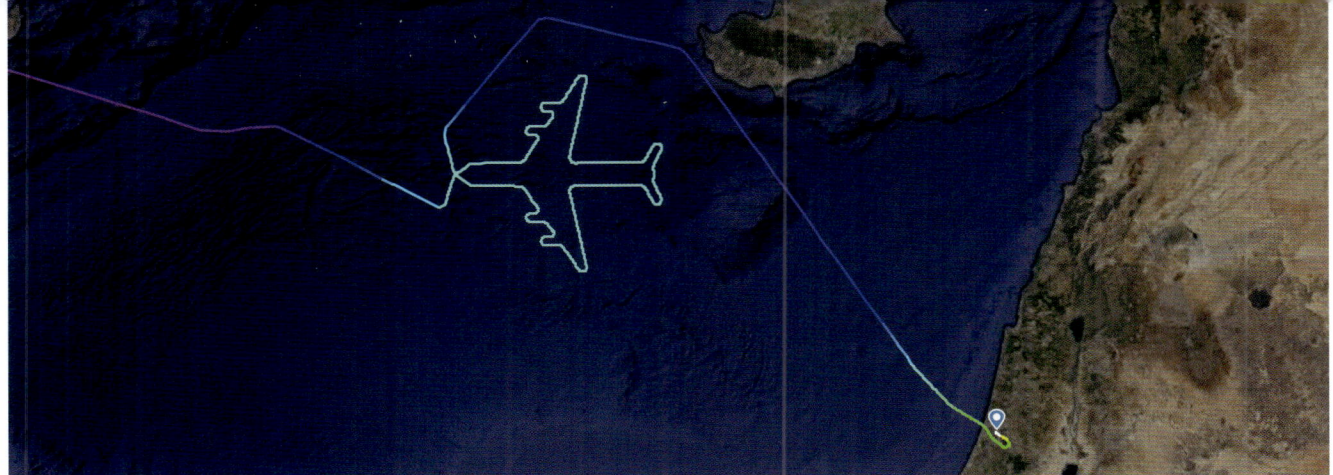

▲ Outline of the 747 in the sky, as seen on Flightradar24

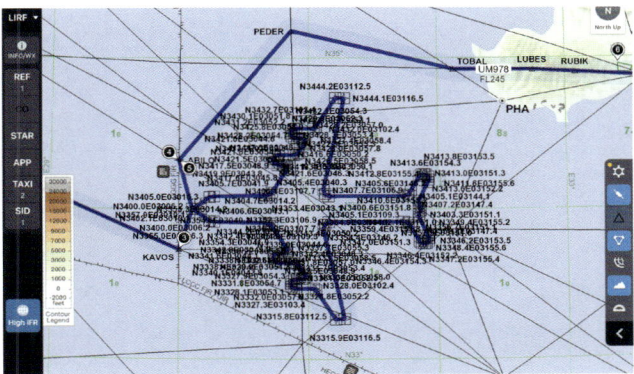

▲ As seen on pilots' navigation software
▼ Buongiorno Roma!

▲ Members of Israel's Orthodox Jewish community join in the fun

Desert Soliloquy

▲ Thai 747 skin recycled into keyrings, one small square at a time

▲ I had many great flights on United 747s, sad to see them here

The desert is Jetliner Country. It's where they come for test flying, training, maintenance, storage, and finally, scrapping. Some, most notably the Tristars out of Lockheed's Palmdale factory, were even born here. The wide-open clear skies are perfect for putting new pilots or new planes through their paces. And the wide-open desert floor is cheap for the enormous amount of land needed to park hundreds of jets, each with a wingspan of 70 metres.

The desert is arid, timeless. But there is an abundance of magic out here. The names themselves hint at magic and poetry – Needles, Flagstaff, Medicine Bow, Joshua Tree, Coachella. Even the names of military and government facilities manage to pack a romantic suggestion of mystery – Groom Lake, Vandenberg, March, Miramar. The Mojave Air & Spaceport. Area 51 is out here, plenty of room for the space programme of an alien species to roam out here. Mushroom clouds from 100 atmospheric nuclear tests rose out of the desert

▲ Surprise! It is possible to enter the passeger cabin through the nose gear and lower avionics bay

▲ First class on an old Qantas machine

▲ I wonder if ever sat in one of these seats before?

Nevada Test Site in the 1950s, visible from downtown hotels in Las Vegas and were tourist attractions.

Standing in the scrapyards of Marana, Kingman, Tucson, Mojave, the sky looks empty, infinite in its vastness. In fact, high overhead up in that bright dark blue are gigantic air corridors for jets dropping into southern California from all over the US – widebodies of Delta from Atlanta and American from Miami or Dallas plying the southern route, patrician United and jetBlue from New York, and heavies that have been cruising for ten hours or more coming in from London, Abu Dhabi, Tokyo. Way up above that, space lanes for Virgin Galactic, Space X, NASA, and a bit of black ops.

On the desert floor, the huge ships of the air come into harbour, for storage in times of economic hardship, to be reactivated when the price of oil drops, the stock exchange rises, or the pandemic subsides. But most will never leave. As the value of the components – avionics,

▲ Many components and systems will fly again in other 747s

moving parts, interior fittings – exceeds that of the intact aircraft, the cutter's torch looms.

That midday sun! The clarity of the light brings mountains that are hundreds of miles away almost within reach. The hot wind is as dry as a bone, without a hint of humidity, so, rather than exhausting, it is almost exhilarating in its intensity. (That said, on the hottest days, old desert hands go to work early, by eight in the morning, and knock off early, around two, to escape the worst of its ravages.)

The old birds sit, gradually shedding parts and looking less and less like their old selves, surrounded by mountains of inventory. Some of it is piled up by type in sheds (flight instruments, control wheels, buckling folders full of weight and balance graphs), or still sits in situ in amputated cockpits after the rest of the plane is in the smelter, surrounded by a silent audience of food trolleys and shrinkwrapped blankets going pale in the sun.

It's a fitting retirement – planes everywhere, nice weather, the occasional visit by spotters to pass the time. Life is good in Jetliner Country!

▲ This United 747 was retired in the Rhapsody Blue livery before the merger with Continental

▲ Just for now, this 747 is all mine

Afterword

Many of the 747 fleets detailed in this book were still flying at the time of writing and designing this book, but by the time of the book's completion, many, including Qantas and KLM on the very same day, and British Airways, Virgin Atlantic, Corsair and Air-India, have announced that due to the close-to-complete shutdown of air travel and ongoing uncertainty resulting from the COVID-19 coronavirus pandemic, their 747 fleets will not return to the skies. It's a cruel blow for the jumbo, which more than any other aircraft, changed the world. The Jet Age jump-started with the 707 at the end of the 1950s, but for comparison, a roundtrip from London to New York on Pan Am in 1958 was £250, and buying a house in London was £800, so flying remained the preserve of the very rich for at least a decade. It took the 747 to connect the masses, and deserved a better send-off.

In a normal world, Qantas would have flown their last 747 on domestic legs packed with well-wishers for a solid week, with news crews and adoring crowds remembering their first trip overseas turning out at every stop. Corsair was already making farewell plans a year in advance for their final trio of almost-timed-out ex-United birds. And the greatest loss of all, British Airways, who loved the jumbo more than any other airline except perhaps Japan Airlines, with dozens of classic -100s and -200Bs followed by an armada of 57 747-400s flying to six continents in six decades, with 30 still in service in 2019 after most delivery customers had retired the fleet. At the time of going to print, the training department have announced the end of all 747 training, including recency checks for the existing crew pool, a de facto permanent grounding for the fleet, without a chance to say goodbye. Even Qantas got a lap of honour over Sydney harbour.

But in a vitally important way, this is the 747's finest hour. The grounding of at least two-thirds of the world's passenger flying has evaporated an enormous volume of underfloor cargo capacity, and the pandemic itself generates additional payloads for emergency supplies such as PPE (personal protective equipment) and medicines. The 286 747 freighters currently in service are flying an average of 15 hours a day, round the clock. Every other target on FlightRadar24 is has that unmistakable outline, wings more aggressively swept, four bumps on the leading edge instead of two. Airline barely known to the public (Silk Way Airlines, Air Bridge Cargo, TransAVIAexport) and cargo divisions of big name airlines (Cathay Pacific, Korean Air, Nippon Cargo Airlines) alike are flying their 747 freighters til the paint comes off.

The 747 has always come to our rescue in our hour of need, such as the evacuation of Darwin on Christmas Day in 1974 following Cyclone Tracy, or water bomber conversions fighting raging fires in climate hot spots. Or just in the every day but vital work of delivering our friends and family, our possessions, our pets, and even our spaceships to all corners of the planet, maintaining the 'physical internet' of moving people and things. Thank you Boeing and thank you 747.

Experiencing The Passion

I am proud to collaborate with Sam on this book, as I share his passion for the 747, the greatest plane ever built. Put it this way. Having been born in Sydney to Australian parents, just shy of my eleventh birthday, my dear mother sat me down on the front steps of our house and told me my father, a space hardware engineer, had been offered a job in London, and how would I feel about us moving there. I thought to myself, to get there, we will definitely have to fly on a 747. I looked her in the eye and said, I think we should do it – cheerfully throwing land of birth, school friends and family under the bus. All for one ride on a 747.

Two of my most memorable airline trips were both on 747-200Bs on the Kangaroo Route. Even though I was just a kid with only the one Qantas flight for comparison, 1980s Thai International via Delhi and Bangkok had something really special about it – the vivid purple and pink cheatline, orchids everywhere, beautiful and kind cabin crew... I still have the keyring they gave me! And Greek national carrier Olympic Airways in the 1990s with a night stop in Athens on the way out. I was up and out in pre-dawn darkness for the twice-weekly 0700 departure by 747 from the old Hellinikon airport to Singapore, Sydney and Melbourne. Olympic had been founded by Greek shipping magnate Aristotle Onassis and somehow retained a flavour of those fashionable years, with a very old school terminal in Athens (steps instead of jetbridges) and bas relief brass artwork on the bulkheads in business class. Very exotic – and even more so today than at the time. Thank you Thai International and Olympic Airways!

The improved fuel burn of big twins that save emissions and money are an obvious evolution, but don't pack the same emotional punch. I really miss the 747 on these long flights, and I am grateful for the chance to remember some of them in this book. Thanks Sam and thanks 747!